DATE DUE

	MAR 1 1 2008

Medicine

Other Books of Related Interest:

Opposing Viewpoints Series

Alternative Medicine

Biomedical Ethics

Stem Cells

At Issue Series

DNA Databases

"Congress shall make
no law . . . abridging
the freedom of speech,
or of the press."

First Amendment to the U.S. Constitution

The basic foundation of our democracy is the First Amendment guarantee of freedom of expression. The Opposing Viewpoints series is dedicated to the concept of this basic freedom and the idea that it is more important to practice it than to enshrine it.

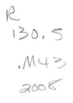

OPPOSING
VIEWPOINTS®
SERIES

Medicine

Louise I. Gerdes, Book Editor

GREENHAVEN PRESS

An imprint of Thomson Gale, a part of The Thomson Corporation

THOMSON
------- ✶ -------
GALE

Detroit • New York • San Francisco • New Haven, Conn. • Waterville, Maine • London

THOMSON
GALE

Christine Nasso, *Publisher*
Elizabeth Des Chenes, *Managing Editor*

© 2008 The Gale Group.

Star logo is a trademark and Gale and Greenhaven Press are registered trademarks used herein under license.

For more information, contact:
Greenhaven Press
27500 Drake Rd.
Farmington Hills, MI 48331-3535
Or you can visit our Internet site at http://www.gale.com

LIBRARY OF CONGRESS CATALOGING-IN-PUBLICATION DATA

Medicine / Louise Gerdes, book editor.
    p. cm. -- Opposing Viewpoints
    Includes bibliographical references and index.
    ISBN-13: 978-0-7377-3759-2 (hardcover)
    ISBN-13: 978-0-7377-3760-8 (pbk.)
    1. Medicine. 2. Medicine--United States. 3. Social medicine--United States.
    4. Medicine--Public opinion. I. Gerdes, Louise I., 1953-
    R130.5.M43 2008
    610--dc22
    2007031325

ISBN-10: 0-7377-3759-X (hardcover)
ISBN-10: 0-7377-3760-3 (pbk.)

Printed in the United States of America
10 9 8 7 6 5 4 3 2 1

Contents

Chapter 4: What Is the Future of Medicine?

Why Consider
Opposing Viewpoints?

"The only way in which a human being can make some approach to knowing the whole of a subject is by hearing what can be said about it by persons of every variety of opinion and studying all modes in which it can be looked at by every character of mind. No wise man ever acquired his wisdom in any mode but this."

John Stuart Mill

In our media-intensive culture it is not difficult to find differing opinions. Thousands of newspapers and magazines and dozens of radio and television talk shows resound with differing points of view. The difficulty lies in deciding which opinion to agree with and which "experts" seem the most credible. The more inundated we become with differing opinions and claims, the more essential it is to hone critical reading and thinking skills to evaluate these ideas. Opposing Viewpoints books address this problem directly by presenting stimulating debates that can be used to enhance and teach these skills. The varied opinions contained in each book examine many different aspects of a single issue. While examining these conveniently edited opposing views, readers can develop critical thinking skills such as the ability to compare and contrast authors' credibility, facts, argumentation styles, use of persuasive techniques, and other stylistic tools. In short, the Opposing Viewpoints series is an ideal way to attain the higher-level thinking and reading skills so essential in a culture of diverse and contradictory opinions.

In addition to providing a tool for critical thinking, Opposing Viewpoints books challenge readers to question their own strongly held opinions and assumptions. Most people form their opinions on the basis of upbringing, peer pressure, and personal, cultural, or professional bias. By reading carefully balanced opposing views, readers must directly confront new ideas as well as the opinions of those with whom they disagree. This is not to simplistically argue that everyone who reads opposing views will—or should—change his or her opinion. Instead, the series enhances readers' understanding of their own views by encouraging confrontation with opposing ideas. Careful examination of others' views can lead to the readers' understanding of the logical inconsistencies in their own opinions, perspective on why they hold an opinion, and the consideration of the possibility that their opinion requires further evaluation.

Evaluating Other Opinions

To ensure that this type of examination occurs, Opposing Viewpoints books present all types of opinions. Prominent spokespeople on different sides of each issue as well as well-known professionals from many disciplines challenge the reader. An additional goal of the series is to provide a forum for other, less-known, or even unpopular viewpoints. The opinion of an ordinary person who has had to make the decision to cut off life support from a terminally ill relative, for example, may be just as valuable and provide just as much insight as a medical ethicist's professional opinion. The editors have two additional purposes in including these less-known views. One, the editors encourage readers to respect others' opinions—even when not enhanced by professional credibility. It is only by reading or listening to and objectively evaluating others' ideas that one can determine whether they are worthy of consideration. Two, the inclusion of such viewpoints encourages the important critical thinking skill of objectively evaluating an author's credentials and bias. This evaluation will illuminate an author's reasons for taking a particular stance on an issue and will aid in readers' evaluation of the author's ideas.

It is our hope that these books will give readers a deeper understanding of the issues debated and an appreciation of the complexity of even seemingly simple issues when good and honest people disagree. This awareness is particularly important in a democratic society such as ours in which people enter into public debate to determine the common good. Those with whom one disagrees should not be regarded as enemies but rather as people whose views deserve careful examination and may shed light on one's own.

Thomas Jefferson once said that "difference of opinion leads to inquiry, and inquiry to truth." Jefferson, a broadly educated man, argued that "if a nation expects to be ignorant and free . . . it expects what never was and never will be." As individuals and as a nation, it is imperative that we consider the opinions of others and examine them with skill and discernment. The Opposing Viewpoints series is intended to help readers achieve this goal.

David L. Bender and Bruno Leone,
Founders

Introduction

> *"Physician report cards are one tool in the toolbox for measuring and improving the quality of medical care. . . . It's very hard to create a reliable, valid, reproducible report card. On the other hand, once you give doctors good information about how they stack up relative to a peer group, get out of the way because they'll trample you on the way to change." —David B. Nash, MD, MBA, chairman of the Department of Health Policy, Jefferson Medical College, Philadelphia, PA*

The United States is a nation that champions consumer choice. Indeed, many American consumers consult product report cards to decide which products and services are best. Discerning consumers, in turn, motivate industries to make their products and services better and safer. The medical "industry," however, has largely been exempt from consumer market forces. "Most Americans," writes journalist David Wessel, "know very little about choosing, say, a heart surgeon. They simply take their primary-care physician's advice or blindly pick a surgeon from those covered by their insurance plan."

Public reporting on the quality of medicine in the United States is growing. Several publications, such as *US News & World Report* and *Consumer Reports*, now identify the "100 best hospitals" or highest-quality health plans; however, only a handful of states have made physician-specific report cards available to consumers. While the public has generally embraced public reporting on products and services, physician-

and hospital-specific report cards remain controversial. As is true of many debates concerning medicine, commentators fall into three general camps: those who believe public report cards improve medicine, those who believe their use is limited or unreliable, and those who believe report cards actually threaten the quality of medicine.

Consumer advocates argue that patients should not have to rely on guesswork to distinguish good doctors from bad. "If you were going to have [a particular] procedure, would you rather go to a doctor who has done two in the last year or done 42?" asks Arthur Levin, director of New York's Center for Medical Consumers. If consumers had access to the same kind of ratings for doctors as they do when they buy a car, the market demand would improve the quality of medical care, advocates assert. This has indeed been the case for hospitals in New York, claims medical journalist Sarah Glazer, "where death rates plunged 41 percent after the state began publicizing hospitals' death rates from cardiac bypass surgery." Glazer maintains that "six hospitals publicly acknowledged that the performance report had spurred them to start quality improvements." Health-care consultant Michael L. Millenson reports, for example, that Winthrop-University Hospital in Mineola, New York, "was stung by its ranking—26th out of the 30 New York hospitals performing cardiac bypass surgery." According to Millenson, "the hospital rose to 15th after recruiting an experienced team of surgeons, upgrading equipment, and improving teamwork between doctors and nurses."

While many agree that public accountability is important, some analysts caution that use of report cards should be limited. "I think the genie is out of the bottle," admits physician and Harvard University professor Arnold M. Epstein. The publicity over reporting, he maintains, has caught the attention of doctors and hospitals and has spurred them to improve the quality of their care. Epstein cautions that, as appealing as report cards may be, "their usefulness will be limited. The public release of performance reports can supplement accreditation, credentialing, well-designed grievance procedures, and focused studies in improving the quality of care, but it cannot replace these other tools." According to Epstein, report cards can never be complete. At best they provide "information on only a few of the many key aspects of health care."

Another concern expressed by like-minded analysts is that report cards are not always reliable. According to physician Yank D. Coble, trustee of the American Medical Association (AMA), "Often, people who have been well-trained and have an unfortunate report are good doctors." Doctor ratings are by their very nature flawed, he argues, because they do not include important factors such as a physician's skill relating to his or her patient. Epstein agrees. To be effective, he claims, report cards must be based on reliable evidence of their effectiveness, must be revised periodically to reflect changes in medical knowledge, and should be standardized and audited to prevent deception. Since statistically reliable physician report cards might prove too expensive, these analysts argue, the validity of report cards is difficult to measure; without standardization, meaningful comparisons are not possible. Epstein recommends prudence. "A single national report is not necessary, and may be a mistake," he cautions. "If our goals, claims, and expectations are appropriate, reporting on quality can become a valuable tool for the health care community."

Still other analysts assert that the consequences of physician report cards outweigh any benefits. Indeed, the most common objection among doctors is that report cards discourage surgeons from operating on higher-risk patients for fear of increasing their mortality rates. Daniel Kessler, a Stanford University economist, claims that report cards do in fact encourage doctors and hospitals to manipulate the report-card system by avoiding sicker patients. To support his conclusions, Kessler cites a 2005 study published in the *Journal of the*

American College of Cardiology. The study's authors discovered that doctors practicing in states that require the public reporting of patient outcomes are holding back potentially life-saving medical care from patients who are at high risk. For example, the authors of the study compared the use of surgery to treat coronary artery disease in Michigan, a state that does not mandate reporting, and in New York, a state that does. Those who had coronary artery surgery in Michigan were, on average, higher-risk patients than those in New York. The rate of mortality in Michigan was correspondingly higher than the mortality rate in New York. However, when the data accounted for this difference, the mortality rates between the two states were equivalent. According to physician Richard N. Fogoros, "While the actual performance of doctors in New York and Michigan appeared to be the same, it appears that doctors and hospitals in New York are optimizing reports of their data by avoiding coronary artery interventions in the highest risk patients." While normal-risk cardiac patients may be a little better off in New York, Fogoros reasons, "If I'm high-risk, I'm considering relocating to Michigan."

The trend toward public health care reporting is growing. While many physicians and hospitals are concerned, "It's a world we're going to have to become comfortable with," writes American Hospital Association spokesman Richard Wade. Whether physician- or hospital-specific report cards will help or harm medicine, however, remains controversial. The authors in *Opposing Viewpoints: Medicine* explore the nature and scope of other issues that confront medicine in the following chapters: What Challenges Confront American Medicine? Is Alternative Medicine Effective? Are New Medical Technologies and Policies Beneficial? and What Is the Future of Medicine?

OPPOSING VIEWPOINTS® SERIES

CHAPTER 1

What Challenges Confront American Medicine?

Chapter Preface

Few question the computer's contribution to the practice of medicine. Veterans Affairs officials can scan bar codes on patient bracelets and medicines and avoid administering the wrong medication or dosage. Kaiser-Permanente doctors can write prescriptions online and access lab tests via e-mail to compare the treatment histories of patients with the same condition. Patients can use the Internet to access articles on recent trends in treatments and fill prescriptions online. However, the computerization of patient health care information has its darker side. Following a series of routine tests, a Florida woman received a mailing from a drug company promoting the sale of a drug to treat her high cholesterol. The teen daughter of a Florida hospital employee accessed the phone numbers of some emergency room patients and as a prank, called and told them that they had been diagnosed with HIV/AIDS. Such incidents have raised concerns about whether there are adequate safeguards in place to protect patient privacy.

The U.S. Congress did address patient privacy early in the new millennium. In April 2003 the Privacy Rule was added to the Health Insurance Portability and Accountability Act of 1996. The rule created a federally mandated right to health information privacy. The Act also imposed restrictions on the use and disclosure of health information and established civil and criminal penalties for violations. It was not until 2005, however, that the Security Rule was added to the Act, setting standards for the protection of electronic health information.

Privacy advocates such as the Electronic Privacy Information Center (EPIC) claim that this regulatory regime for protecting the privacy of electronic health information remains too complex and fragmented. Their concern is that without proper safeguards, many patients fearing unauthorized access and discrimination may not be completely honest with their doctors. "Without trust that the personal, sensitive information they share with their doctors will be handled with some degree of confidentiality," claims Janlori Goldman, director of the Health Privacy Project, "people will not fully participate in their own health care." Although computer records are more easily protected than paper records and adequate technology is available to protect patient privacy, federally mandated security measures only became effective in 2005. "It is too early," EPIC maintains, "to know how doctors, health plans and other entities will interpret and implement the Security Rule."

Opponents of additional government regulation argue that a few isolated, but well publicized, incidents have inflated the problem of health information privacy. Moreover, they assert, the massive volume of online medical information will make it difficult for federal agencies to monitor for violations. Industry self-regulation, they argue, is the best way to protect patient privacy. "The private sector has done a good job of responding to privacy concerns during the seminal growth of electronics commerce," claims Scott Cooper of Hewlett-Packard. "Self-regulation and credible third-party enforcement is the single most important step businesses can take to ensure that consumers' privacy will be respected and protected online," he maintains. Health insurers, hospitals, and medical research groups want to protect patient privacy. They also want groups to be able to obtain health information when necessary. "It is vital that information-sharing continue among health plans and insurers, health-care providers and health-care clearinghouses for purposes of treatment, payment and health-care operations," argues Charles N. Kahn III, president of the Health Insurance Association of America. "Overly restrictive barriers to such exchanges," he reasons, "are potentially harmful to patients."

Advocates on both sides of the controversy continue to debate what policies will best protect patient privacy in the electronic age. The authors in the following chapter examine other challenges that the American medical field faces.

> "At least part of the [racial] disparity [in health care] results from care providers making racist and stereotyped decisions about when and what treatment to offer."

Racism Is a Serious Problem in Modern Medicine

Kai Wright

People of color are less likely to receive quality health care due to racist attitudes among health care providers, claims Kai Wright in the following viewpoint. Those who oppose policies that would address racial health care disparities deny that racism is to blame, Wright maintains. Instead, he argues, opponents perpetuate racism by making claims that the culture and biology of people of color promote behaviors that are destructive to health. Wright, who writes on issues related to race, sex, and health, is author of Soldiers of Freedom: An Illustrated History of African Americans in the Armed Forces.

As you read, consider the following questions:

1. What do Amy Ansell and researcher Jack Geiger claim is the "new racism"?

Kai Wright, "What Your Doctor Won't See . . . ," *ColorLines*, vol. 10, March/April 2007, pp. 19-29. Copyright © 2007 *ColorLines* Magazine. Reproduced by permission.

2. What diseases reflect the most egregious disparities between whites and people of color, in the author's view?

3. How does the assertion that health care differences stem from culture and biology make racial profiling worthwhile for conservatives, in the author's opinion?

For three decades, conservative thinkers have worked mightily to discredit race-based considerations in public policy and cement the belief that America today is, as it should be, a colorblind society. "It really begins in the early '70s," says Bard University sociologist Amy Ansell, author of *New Right, New Racism*. "Conservatives believe that with the civil rights movement the barriers were brought down, and that's when racism ends. At that point, government and society have nothing more to do."

Instead, as [City University of New York (CUNY) researcher Jack] Geiger suggests, the answers are said to lie in changing the behaviors of people of color. Notably, . . . conservative activists do not deny the existence of inequality. To the contrary, says Tarso Luis Ramos, research director of Political Research Associates, a progressive think tank, they nominally share anti-racists' outrage over the gaps. "The rhetoric acknowledges disparities and even decries them on one hand, and on the other hand rejects proposals to reduce these disparities," Ramos says.

The New Racism

A circuitous intellectual route squares this circle of thought. Colorblind ideology rests on two premises: reducing racism to "individual acts of meanness," as Ramos puts it, and blaming unequal outcomes in any given area on the cultural norms of individuals affected. Like Ansell, Ramos traces the "new racism" to the years following the civil rights movement, and in particular the infamous Moynihan Report, which he argues established the idea that Blacks' troubles stem from the destructive devolution of their culture.

In the ensuing years, Ramos says, rightwing thinkers and advocates built on this premise. They stroked America's individualist ethos as they steadily narrowed racism's definition to exclude broad, structural factors. And they drove home the idea that both oppression and liberation lie in individual rather than societal acts—that, where racism is concerned, *I* rather than *we* shall overcome. As a result, efforts like affirmative action are dismissed because they misdirect the burden of fighting racism onto individuals who are not racist, while failing to address the impossibly complicated cultural deficiencies that actually hold people of color back. . . .

"'Colorblind' ideology," says Ramos, "is now the dominant frame for race in America today."

Racial Disparity in Health Care

But one arena in which the colorblind movement has so far failed has been healthcare. In fact, public health has rushed down a directly opposing path on race. Starting in the mid 1980s and rising to a crescendo during the Clinton administration–tenure of Surgeon General David Satcher—the first Black to hold that post—public health has become consumed by questions about racial disparities.

This is in no small part because the evidence is uniquely damning. Since the civil rights movement's close, Blacks in particular have made no progress on what may be the most important measure of social well-being: living to see old age. According to a 2005 paper coauthored by Satcher for a special racial disparities issue of the journal *Health Affairs*, an alarming 40 percent gap between Black and white mortality rates hasn't budged in the last 40 years. In an accompanying article, University of Michigan sociology and epidemiology professor David Williams highlighted specific death trends. Black and white death rates from heart disease were equal in 1950; by 2002, Blacks died 30 percent more often. Blacks had a 10-

percent lower cancer death rate than whites in 1950; now it's 25 percent higher. The infant mortality gap doubled between 1950 and 2002.

As researchers have documented this divide, they've also begun tracking the reasons for it. In 1998, CUNY's Geiger led a massive literature review of the existing information on racial health disparities. His work focused on bias in the delivery of care. Prior to the 1960s, he says, discrimination in the healthcare system was overt and dramatic—segregated hospitals, Black wards housed in dank cellars, emergency rooms turning away dying nonwhite patients. But after Jim Crow's nominal ousting from healthcare, the bias took more nuanced forms that were harder to measure or track. As a result, throughout the 1970s, most information about bias was anecdotal.

In the 1980s, researchers gained access to Medicare data that made possible real comparisons of what sort of care Americans were getting in the post-civil rights era. Medicare leveled the analytical field—everyone had the same insurance—and the program collected a trove of data, allowing researchers to control for a host of factors and isolate race. Suddenly, a flood of studies began documenting disparities in both care and outcomes.

Looking for Explanations

Policymakers have taken notice of all of this. Satcher had the health department target a number of diseases with the most egregious disparities—heart disease, diabetes, and HIV/AIDS, among others—and [former Secretary of Health and Human Services Tommy] Thompson at least nominally maintained those priorities under the Bush administration. Republican and Democratic lawmakers alike have drafted legislation calling for more data and targeted funding, and in 1999, in addition to ordering up the annual National Healthcare Disparities Report, Congress directed the Institute of Medicine (IOM) to prepare a seminal study on health disparities that prescribed policymaking remedies. It's this titanic report that has most animated conservative naysayers.

Released in 2002, the IOM's report rocked the healthcare world. Conventional wisdom had thus far been that racial health disparities were primarily due to access to care, that people of color got sick and died more often because they were more likely to be uninsured or underinsured.

But the IOM study asserted that much more was at play. It declared that even given the same insurance, the same income and the same type of treatment facility, people of color were less likely to receive quality care. The disturbing gap existed across a wide range of treatments—breast cancer screenings, angioplasties, hip fracture repairs, and on and on. Whites were even more likely to get an eye exam than nonwhites.

The IOM cited a host of complex and dynamic causes for this inequality. There were structural factors, such as financial incentives to limit services given to poor patients; communication factors like missing translators or English-only signage and literature; even factors driven by the patients themselves, whose own beliefs and preferences led them to refuse certain types of care or fail to follow doctors' instructions. But what grabbed everyone's attention was the IOM's charge that at least part of the disparity results from care providers making racist and stereotyped decisions about when and what treatment to offer.

"It was a landmark," says Geiger, who contributed to the report. "And the IOM had the resources to publicize it, and the science reporters in the country paid attention—and it confronted the wishful beliefs of both the profession and the public."

Trying to Shift Responsibility

If so, it was a confrontation that conservative thinkers rose to meet.

"What I'm focusing on is this word 'disparity,'" author and psychiatrist Sally Satel told a February 2006 forum on her new book, *The Health Disparities Myth*. "If you look it up in the dictionary, it is a perfectly neutral word. It means difference. But over the last few years, it has taken on another connotation. It has taken on the meaning of that of injustice." Satel and other conservative thinkers make no effort to counter the facts of racial health disparities; their arguments turn on the cause. "We acknowledge that healthcare certainly varies by race" Satel explains, "but we challenge the idea that it varies because of race." . . .

Satel led a chorus of outrage emanating from AEI [American Enterprise Institute] over the IOM's report. Critics set aside the report's range of diagnoses and prescriptions to narrowly focus the debate on those involving racism at the clinician level. And they enhanced the personal responsibility mantra with an equally compelling—and once again familiar—assertion: that focusing on racial justice actually further erodes quality of care by unjustly promoting affirmative action and discouraging doctors from taking race-based cultural and biological factors into account in treatment decisions.

The affirmative-action argument is the most familiar. Satel and AEI have taken particular aim at the IOM's call for policies that get more people of color into the health professions and for more enforcement funding for the health department's Office of Civil Rights. "All agree that it is important to close the gap," a responding AEI press release insisted, "but the report offers some unrealistic, even potentially harmful, solutions that involve turning the disparity issue into a civil-rights problem."

Blaming Race, Not Racism

Interestingly, there exists widespread agreement on all sides of the debate about how the wellness gap plays out. The controversy is what to call this gap—leading to odd semantic jousts like the one surrounding "disparities" versus "differences." To conservatives, the "differences" are value-neutral and stem from natural factors like culture and biology, not political or social ones. As with racial profiling in law enforcement and national security, it's this assertion that makes medical stereotyping worthwhile yet renders considerations of social justice destructive. And as we've also seen in other areas, it's this equation that paves the way to individual and private solutions rather than public ones.

Satel deftly employs a rhetorical slight-of-hand when defending doctors' practice of making treatment decisions about individual patients based on their race. In essays published by both *The Wall Street Journal* and *The New York Times*, she has scoffed at the widespread belief that the Human Genome Project—which established in 2000 that 99.9 percent of human genes are the same—proved race to be a social rather than biological construct.

In the *Times* article, titled "I Am a Racially Profiling Doctor," she compellingly argued that race was an admittedly imperfect but nonetheless crucial clue for doctors making diagnoses and deciding how to treat. "When it comes to practicing medicine, stereotyping often works," she wrote, listing a number of racial patterns that guide her clinical choices. Blacks appear to metabolize antidepressants slower, so she starts all Black patients on low doses; Blacks do less well in Hepatitis C treatment, so she counsels all Black patients on their limited chances of success. "So much of medicine is a guessing game—and race sometimes provides an invaluable clue."

But one woman's clue is another's prejudice. It's the sort of generalizing Satel boasts about that leaves people of color with unequal care. "Discrimination can be a scary term, as it frequently conjures up images of nefarious actors engaging in conscious acts of bigotry," writes University of Maryland health-law scholar Thomas Perez in the IOM report's chapter on civil rights. "Discrimination in today's healthcare marketplace is much more subtle."

University of Minnesota researcher Michelle Van-Ryn led one key study examining those subtleties. Her team surveyed heart patients and doctors involved in 618 encounters at eight New York hospitals in which post-angiogram treatments were discussed. The doctors were overwhelmingly white, and the patients were split roughly evenly between Black and white. Van-Ryn found doctors more likely to hold a host of negative beliefs about the Black patients: They were presumed to be more likely to abuse drugs or alcohol and less likely to be educated, to comply with physicians' instructions, to want an active lifestyle or to participate in cardiac rehab if prescribed. Among low-income Blacks and whites, doctors were far more likely to consider white patients both "pleasant" and "rational" than Black patients. Doctors were even more likely to say the white patients were "the kind of person I could see myself being friends with" than the Black patients.

"Of course, what you're looking at are the classic stereotypes—lazy, uneducated," says Geiger. He argues those stereotypes have shaped care for decades and that public health has consistently found excuses for racial gaps in wellness that have always existed. "The first explanation was that Negroes were biologically inferior. That was replaced gradually by the notion that it's their own fault. They drink, they smoke, they don't live right."

In that sense, Satel's defense of profiling sets up a new twist on an old theme: racism isn't to blame for health disparities, but rather race itself.

"It is long past time to put aside the incendiary claim that racism plays a meaningful role in health status of African-Americans."

Racism Is Not a Serious Problem in Modern Medicine

Sally Satel

In the following viewpoint, Sally Satel argues that health disparities between blacks and whites are not due to racism but to differences in the quality of and access to health care. While hardworking and committed, Satel maintains, doctors who treat black patients are less likely to be board certified in their specialty or have access to specialists. Moreover, she claims, these doctors are less likely to screen for diseases and more likely to manage symptoms when diseases are more advanced. Satel, a scholar at the conservative American Enterprise Institute, is author of The Health Disparities Myth.

As you read, consider the following questions:

1. What did research at Manhattan's Memorial Sloan-Kettering Cancer Center show?

2. What research does Satel cite to support her claim that the capacities of doctors who treat black patients account for part of the health gap?

3. In the author's opinion, what course would best reduce the health gap?

A t a certain point, it became possible to take a snapshot of America's health, complete with vivid details and statistical portraits. Among other things, the snapshot revealed that blacks and whites experience different rates of diabetes, stroke, some cancers and other conditions—and different rates of diagnosis and treatment. And the reason? Plausible answers easily come to mind: genetics, discrepancies in insurance coverage, the availability of medical care and varying patient attitudes toward it. Two years ago, another reason was added: racism.

It was then that the Institute of Medicine (IOM) published "Unequal Treatment," a much-heralded report arguing that doctors—acting deliberately or unconsciously—were giving their minority patients inferior care. The notion that doctors (and thus the workings of the entire health-care system) commit "bias," "prejudice" and "stereotyping"—as the IOM report put it—is now conventional wisdom at many medical schools, philanthropies and health agencies. The Web site of the American Medical Association cites "discrimination at the individual patient-provider level" as a cause of heath-care disparities. Introducing a health bill [in 2003] [former Senate Majority Leader] Sen. Tom Daschle cited the need to correct doctors' "bias," "stereotyping" and "discrimination."

Questioning the Biased-Doctor Model

Skeptics of the biased-doctor model, and I count myself among them, do not dispute the troubling existence of a health gap. But we argue that the examining room is not the place to look for its origins. This is not to suggest that doctor-patient

The Wrong Approach

Whenever someone promises to attack a racial disparity, I worry. Because, inevitably, the problem turns out to be rooted in something other than race, so that taking a race-oriented approach results in more discrimination than you had to start out with. . . .

It is very unlikely that the right way to address a racial or ethnic health disparity is through a racial or ethnic approach. These are health issues, not civil-rights issues. There are millions of people who need better health care, and they come in all colors. It is wrong to pass a bill that will encourage the health-care system to focus more on some racial or ethnic groups than others.

Roger Clegg, "Unhealthy Disparities,"
National Review, *April 20, 2004. www.nationalreview.com.*

relationships are free of clinical uncertainty and miscommunication; they are not. But their relative importance is probably modest and remains hard to gauge, especially when compared with access to care and quality of care—both of which have undisputed and sizable effects.

This argument just got a big boost from researchers at Manhattan's Memorial Sloan-Kettering Cancer Center and the Center for the Study of Health Care Change in Washington. They showed that white and black patients, on average, do not even visit the same population of physicians—making the idea of preferential treatment by individual doctors a far less compelling explanation for disparities in health. They show, too, that a higher proportion of the doctors that black patients tend to see may not be in a position to provide optimal care.

The dramatic finding, published in the *New England Journal of Medicine*, should incite a fundamental shift in thinking. Whether it actually does that is another matter, so entrenched are the pieties about America's racist inclinations.

The research team, led by Dr. Peter Bach, examined more than 150,000 visits by black and white Medicare recipients to 4,355 primary-care physicians nationwide in 2001. It found that the vast majority of visits by black patients were made to a small group of physicians—80% of their visits were made to 22% of all the physicians in the study. Is it possible, the researchers asked, that doctors who disproportionately treat black patients are different from other doctors? Do their clinical qualifications and their resources differ?

Explaining Racial Disparities

The answer is yes. Physicians of any race who disproportionately treat African-American patients, the study notes, were less likely to have passed a demanding certification exam in their specialty than the physicians treating white patients. More important, they were more likely to answer "not always" when asked whether they had access to high-quality colleague-specialists to whom they could refer their patients (e.g., cardiologists, gastroenterologists), or to nonemergency hospital services, diagnostic imaging and ancillary services such as home health aid.

These patterns reflect geographic distribution. Primary-care physicians who lack board certification and who encounter obstacles to specialized services are more likely to practice in areas where blacks receive their care—namely, poorer neighborhoods, as measured by the median income.

Dr. Bach and his colleagues suggest that these differences play a considerable role in racial disparities in health care and health status. They make a connection between well-established facts: that physicians who are not board certified are (a) less likely to follow screening recommendations and

(b) more likely to manage symptoms rather than pursue diagnosis. Thus rates of screening for breast and cervical cancer or high blood pressure are lower among black patients than white, and black patients are more likely to receive a diagnosis when their diseases are at an advanced stage. Limited access to specialty services similarly put black patients at a disadvantage.

The Bach study is the first to examine physicians' access to specialty care and nonemergency hospital admissions in light of the race of the patients they treat. As for the notion that that the capacities of doctors who treat black patients may account for some part of the health gap, earlier evidence for it has been hiding in plain sight.

For example, a 2002 study in the *Journal of the American Medical Association* found that physicians working for managed-care plans in which black patients were heavily enrolled provided lower-quality care to all patients. A report in the *American Journal of Public Health* in 2000 found that black patients undergoing cardiovascular surgery had poorer access to high-quality surgeons. Similarly, Dartmouth researchers have shown that African-Americans tend to live in areas or seek care in regions where the quality for all patients, black and white, is at a lower level.

Facing Challenges in Black Communities

It is important to recognize that many of the physicians working in black communities are hardworking, committed individuals who make considerable financial sacrifices to serve their patients. As Dr. Bach's team notes, they deliver more charity care than doctors who mostly treat white patients and derive a higher volume of their practice revenue from Medicaid, a program whose fees are notoriously low. They are often solo practitioners who scramble to make good referrals for their patients but who are stymied by a dearth of well-trained colleagues and by limited entrée to professional networks with advanced diagnostic techniques.

It is long past time to put aside the incendiary claim that racism plays a meaningful role in the health status of African-Americans. The health gap is assuredly real. But growing evidence suggests that the most promising course is to get well-trained doctors into low-income and rural neighborhoods and enable them to provide the best care for their patients—something they will do, it somehow needs to be said, without prejudice.

| "A survey of physicians showed that over 76 percent believed malpractice litigation affected their ability to provide quality healthcare."

Medical Malpractice Litigation Threatens American Medicine

Sherman Joyce

The medical malpractice liability system is costly and makes it difficult for physicians to provide quality health care, claims Sherman Joyce in the following viewpoint. The purpose of large jury awards is to deter shoddy medical practices, but this system has not improved patient safety, he claims. In fact, Joyce argues, some doctors order unnecessary tests and procedures to protect themselves in the event of litigation. The high cost of litigation leads to rising malpractice insurance costs that also hurt patients because these costs drive many physicians from practice, he maintains. Joyce is president of the American Tort Reform Association.

As you read, consider the following questions:

1. According to Joyce, how much did jury awards increase between 1997 and 2003?

Sherman Joyce, testimony before the Subcommittee on Health, Committee on Energy and Commerce, United States House of Representatives Regarding Current Issues Related to Medical Liability Reform, February 10, 2005. Reproduced by permission of the author.

2. According to the Health Coalition on Liability and Access, what percentage of Americans believe doctors are leaving their practices due to unaffordable malpractice premiums?

3. What is the centerpiece of California's Medical Injury Compensation Reform Act, in the author's opinion?

There is no doubt that the American healthcare system is the finest in the world. We have the best doctors, hospitals, and medical schools. American pharmaceutical companies are the engine of innovation in creating life-saving medicines. America has conquered polio, developed cures for serious diseases that were once death sentences, and created technologies and therapies that have not only improved the American people's health, but also the world's.

Unfortunately, we also know that our healthcare system costs are a major issue for consumers and elected officials, with annual costs increasing at double digit rates. This increase threatens the very greatness of our healthcare system, and ultimately the American people's access to world class medical care. While elected officials at the federal and state level discuss possible solutions to this problem, be they medical savings accounts or a single-payer healthcare system, one of the contributing factors to the healthcare cost problem is the crisis in our medical liability system. ATRA [American Tort Reform Association] believes that Congress should consider reforms to our medical liability system as one of the critical elements to reform our healthcare system.

An Inadequate Liability System

An effective medical liability system should provide predictability and fairness, guided by the over-arching principle of fairly compensating those who are truly injured by medical negligence.

Unfortunately, our medical liability system comes up short.

In our system, costs are escalating astronomically. According to the Physicians Insurers Association of America, a trade association composed of 50 insurance companies owned by doctors and dentists, the median medical liability jury award nearly doubled from $157,000 in 1997 to $300,000 in 2003. The average award also increased from $347,134 in 1997 to $430,727 in 2002. The growth in settlements followed this trend, with the median settlement increasing from $100,000 in 1997 to $200,000 in 2002. Average settlements increased from $212,861 in 1997 to $322,544 in 2002.

In addition to sharp escalation in costs, however, the medical liability system is highly inefficient. Prompt and full compensation to injured plaintiffs are the exception and not the rule. A full 70 percent of medical liability claims result in no payment to the plaintiffs. Of the 5.8 percent of claims that do go to a jury verdict, defendants won 86.2 percent of the time, with an average cost to defend such lawsuits of $87,720 per claim.

In addition to being expensive and inefficient, the system does a poor job of promoting patient safety. Only 1.53 percent of patients injured by medical error file claims and most claims that are filed do not involve medical malpractice. Such a system plainly fails to serve the interests of all parties to litigation.

The Costs of Defensive Medicine

Doctors routinely order unnecessary tests and procedures to guard against the possibility of litigation in the aftermath of a bad outcome. According to a study published in the *Quarterly Journal of Economics,* the excess cost of defensive medicine contributes $50 billion annually to the cost of our healthcare system. Through programs such as Medicare and Medicaid, the federal government pays tens of billions of dollars to pay the costs associated with defensive medicine. According to a recent HHS [U.S. Department of Health and Human Services] report, between $28.6 and $47.5 billion per year in taxpayer funds is spent indirectly subsidizing this system. These increased costs in a financially overburdened healthcare system reduce both the access to and quality of healthcare. The root of this problem is an unpredictable litigation system in which the volatile nature of jury verdicts provides no clear signals and predictability to healthcare providers and insurers.

The current costs of the litigation system impose burdens on taxpayers and individual physicians. This compromises innovation in delivering improvements to patient safety. The result is a medical liability system that is too costly, offers little deterrent value, and, at best, does little to promote improvements in patient safety. For example, the American Hospital Association has reported that 45 percent of hospitals have lost physicians and/or reduced coverage in emergency departments due to the medical liability crisis. Stories about individual physicians are equally compelling. For example, after serving 30 years as medical director for Forsyth County Emergency Medical Services of North Carolina, Dr. Lew Stringer resigned his position in 2003 due to the lack of availability of affordable malpractice insurance. And in Missouri, family physician Dr. Donald Maples closed his practice after serving the community of Kirksville for 14 years because of the high cost of his medical liability insurance. Commenting on his experience, Dr. Maples said, "I expected to be here until I was in my mid-60s, but the reality is that I can no longer really truly afford to do this."

The Impact on Patient Access to Healthcare

A survey of physicians showed that over 76 percent believed malpractice litigation affected their ability to provide quality healthcare. According to the American Medical Association (AMA), 20 states are in the midst of a healthcare liability crisis, while another 25 states show problem signs that indicate a

crisis is imminent. ATRA believes that this litigation environment has resulted in many physicians stopping the practice of medicine, abandoning high-risk parts of their practices, or moving their practices to other states. The public has taken notice, as well. According to a nationwide survey commissioned by the Health Coalition on Liability and Access, 82 percent of Americans believe doctors are leaving their practices due to unaffordable malpractice premiums caused by excessive litigation.

For example, on January 10, 2005, Mercy Hospital of Wilkes-Barre, Pennsylvania, stopped delivering babies because of the retirement of several OB/GYNs [obstetrician/gynecologists] due to the high cost of medical liability insurance. Pennsylvania has been hit hard by the medical liability crisis, with a 2004 poll suggesting that one in four patients have changed doctors in the Keystone state due to the medical liability crisis.

In early January [2005], President Bush visited Southern Illinois to discuss the medical liability crisis. The President pointed out that Madison and St. Clair Counties had lost about 160 doctors over the last two years due to the medical liability crisis. High-risk specialists have been particularly hard hit; in 2004, the last two brain neurosurgeons in Southern Illinois resigned their posts at Neurological Associates of Southern Illinois because their malpractice insurance premiums were approaching $300,000.

Examining Proven Policies

Fortunately, there are proven policy changes that Congress can enact to abate this liability crisis. These laws can ensure Americans will continue to enjoy high quality medical care. At the same time, these reforms will protect the rights of patients in cases of true medical negligence. As Congress contemplates a legislative remedy, ATRA believes that any such legislation should apply to all defendants in healthcare actions. Doing so will ensure that all parties in a claim are treated equitably in the civil justice system.

The solution to the medical liability problem was devised over 25 years ago in California with reforms called the Medical Injury Compensation Reform Act, better known as MICRA. Like much of the United States today, California experienced a medical liability crisis in the early 1970s. By 1972, a sharp increase in litigiousness ensured that California medical malpractice insurance carriers were paying claims well in excess of dollars that they collected in premiums. The crisis continued to worsen. By 1975, two major malpractice carriers in Southern California notified physicians that their coverage would not be renewed. At the same time, another insurer announced that premiums for Northern California physicians would increase by 380 percent. In response to the crisis, then-Governor Jerry Brown called the California Legislature into special session to develop solutions. The result was MICRA.

Signed by Governor Brown in 1975, MICRA's centerpiece is a single cap of $250,000 on noneconomic damages. Other provisions of MICRA include: (1) allowing collateral source benefits to be introduced into evidence; (2) permitting the periodic payment of judgments in excess of $50,000; (3) allowing patients and physicians to contract for binding arbitration; and (4) limiting attorney contingency fees according to a sliding scale.

Evidence indicates that MICRA's success has stabilized insurance rates in California by limiting overall damages and by substantially diminishing the unpredictability—the volatility—of judgments. . . .

MICRA has ensured that those injured by medical negligence receive fair compensation, but it also has ensured that the market for medical liability insurance has remained stable and affordable. As a result, California has been largely immune from the liability crisis endemic to other states.

Answering the Opposition

Opponents of medical liability reform claim that the "access to healthcare" problem is a myth and that MICRA-style reforms are not the solution to rising malpractice premiums. One of the most common arguments they advance is that malpractice rates are increasing because insurance companies are making up for investment losses suffered in the stock market bubble in the late 1990s. They further argue that insurance carriers are gouging doctors with rate increases to boost profits.

A brief examination of the evidence, however, suggests otherwise. A report by the investment and asset management firm Brown Brothers Harriman examined the investment mix of medical liability insurance carriers and the effect those investments had on premiums. The Brown Brothers report found no relationship between losses suffered by carriers in the stock market and rising premiums, "As medical malpractice companies did not have an unusual amount invested in equities and since they invested these monies in a reasonable market-like fashion, we conclude that the decline in equity valuations is not the cause of rising medical malpractice premiums."

In addition, more than 60 percent of physicians obtain insurance through physician owned and operated companies. These companies began to form in the 1970s when commercial carriers were exiting the medical liability insurance market due to unexpected losses, leaving healthcare providers no other options but to form their own insurance companies. These companies compete with commercial carriers and return excess revenue to policy holders, the owners of the companies. The contention that malpractice premiums are increasing in an effort to boost profits is, in essence, asking us to believe that a majority of doctors are "gouging" themselves and picking their own pockets. A reasonable examination can reach only one conclusion: medical liability insurance premiums are increasing because of higher costs and instability of our current litigation system, which does not allow carriers to accurately predict future losses and provide reasonable pricing of liability policies. Insurers price their product on cost and risk. It is logical to infer that a medical liability system that is more expensive and more volatile will necessarily be more expensive to insure.

Looking for Answers

A 2003 Government Accounting Office (GAO) study examined the impact of the medical liability system on access to healthcare. The report acknowledged that states that limit noneconomic damages have enjoyed a lower rate of increase in medical liability insurance rates than states with more limited reforms. As our opponents are quick to point out, however, the report also alleged that there is little evidence to suggest that states with no limits on damages have a healthcare access problem.

The report is incomplete. GAO examined only a limited number of states, 5, and not the entire 18 then in crisis, as identified by the AMA at the time that the GAO conducted its examination. It has never been ATRA's position that the effects of the medical liability crisis are uniform. Many variables drive the crisis, including the type of medical specialty, the physician's location (urban, rural, or suburban), and the overall litigation environment of a particular region. In some areas and among some specialties, the effects of the current crisis are minimal; in other areas, and many other specialties, the effects of the crisis are profound.

Members of Congress should examine the medical liability system and assess the effects that current cost escalation and litigation will have on the future. ATRA believes such an examination inevitably leads to the conclusion that the costs associated with the current system are unsustainable and that MICRA-style reforms must be enacted. Such reforms are in the best interests of patients, taxpayers, physicians, and plaintiffs. And these reforms should apply to all defendants in litigation. As Californians can attest, strong medical liability reforms create a system that strikes the correct balance between fairly compensating victims of medical negligence with a liability market that stabilizes premiums for physicians. This reform will go a long way toward enhancing and protecting access to healthcare. Lawmakers should not wait to act until a full-blown crisis is verified by a government report. It is the responsibility of elected officials to take remedial and, if necessary, preventive action to ensure that such a crisis never occurs.

"*Far more effective than an arbitrary cap on damages would be a more systematic effort to weed out bad doctors and prevent malpractice in the first place.*"

Medical Malpractice Reform Will Not Improve American Medicine

Sasha Polakow-Suransky

Putting a cap on medical malpractice awards will not improve patient safety, claims Sasha Polakow-Suransky in the following viewpoint. In fact, he argues, large awards for pain and suffering deter bad doctors. High malpractice insurance claims are due to economic decisions made by insurance companies, not increasing jury awards, Polakow-Suransky maintains. Policies that prevent medical malpractice in the first place are better for medicine than policies that punish the victim's right to sue for damages, he reasons. Polakow-Suransky is associate editor for the journal Foreign Affairs.

As you read, consider the following questions:

1. What does Polakow-Suransky claim is largely responsible for rising medical malpractice premiums?

2. According to the author, what are some of the injuries that cannot be quantified in economic terms?

3. In the author's opinion, what remedies to rising medical malpractice premiums do Massachusetts, Indiana, and Louisiana employ?

For the third time in as many decades, doctors across the country are protesting rising medical-malpractice insurance premiums. The American Medical Association (AMA) is promoting its long-standing goal of medical-liability reform in the shape of a $250,000 cap on "pain and suffering" (noneconomic) damages in malpractice cases.

President [George W.] Bush's AMA-backed proposal to cap pain and suffering damages at $250,000 will satisfy the AMA's desire to shield doctors from liability while curtailing maimed patients' rights to sue. But in the end it is more likely to line the pockets of insurance companies than reduce rates for doctors.

Depending on whose statistics you use, the median jury award for malpractice ranges from $125,000 to $1 million. The Physician Insurers Association of America reports that claim payments of more than $1 million have increased from less than 2 percent in 1990 to almost 8 percent in 2001, driving the median up from $150,000 to more than $300,000. Contrary to insurance-industry claims, however, overall medical-malpractice payouts have not increased substantially. During market downturns, insurers set aside vast reserves to pay anticipated claims, counting these reserves as "incurred losses"—even while these funds accrue investment income. But excluding these set-asides, actual insurance-company payouts increased only 15 percent from 1998 to 2001, according to Americans for Insurance Reform (AIR)—far less than premium increases in most states.

What Drives Rising Premiums

Medical-malpractice law is a lucrative industry, as many a phone book cover will attest. But contrary to the administration's line, increasing jury awards are not single-handedly driving premiums through the roof. Rather, a steep decline in insurers' projected investment income is largely responsible for rising rates. Medical-malpractice insurers do not invest heavily in stocks; in fact, approximately 80 percent to 90 percent of their investments are in the bond market, and bond income has been declining. Moreover, insurance companies are technically barred from recovering past losses by raising premiums, an argument the AMA parrots to dismiss claims that insurance companies are at fault. But insurance companies do regularly raise rates based on projected investment losses. For medical-malpractice insurers, investment income represents a far greater share of profits than in other lines of coverage due to the long lag (up to 10 years) between premium payments and claim payouts. And when investment income evaporates, it hits hard. AIR's J. Robert Hunter, an actuary and former Texas insurance commissioner, tracked premiums and insurance-industry investment returns over the last 30 years. He found that each of the three malpractice insurance "crises" directly coincided with declining insurance investment returns.

Insurance competition in the 1990s, followed by steep drops in interest rates, drove premiums up sharply. As *The Wall Street Journal* exhaustively documented in 2002, malpractice insurers launched a price war in the 1990s after major companies realized they had set aside too much capital in loss reserves. As large insurers such as St. Paul Cos. released reserves, medical malpractice suddenly appeared immensely profitable and multiple new companies entered the market,

Punishing the Victims

What capping damages does is punish those individuals who have already suffered horrors like paralysis, brain damage and the loss of a limb by placing an arbitrary ceiling on their compensation, regardless of the judgment of a jury, while failing to address the underlying problem of medical malpractice. Essentially, damage-award caps are Band-aids that cause bleeding.

Diana Degette, "A Band-Aid That Causes Bleeding,"
CQ Researcher: Medical Malpractice, *February 13, 2003.*

aggressively undercutting the larger companies and one another. The result was a bargain for doctors and a brewing storm for insurers. As claims piled up, the low rates no longer proved adequate to cover costs. The largest insurer, St. Paul, left the market. To add to the mess, falling interest rates meant declining yields on bonds. To stay afloat, insurers had to raise rates. "When interest yields decrease, rates must increase," Jim Hurley, a medical-malpractice expert at the actuary firm Tillinghast-Towers Perrin, told the Senate Committee on Appropriations in March [2003].

The Hardest Hit Are High-Risk Specialists

While general practitioners have not been particularly hard hit by rising premiums, neurosurgeons, obstetricians and other high-risk specialists have seen rates soar. According to the trade journal *Medical Liability Monitor*, annual premiums for obstetrician/gynecologists in Las Vegas increased from $79,000 in 2001 to nearly $108,000 in 2002, while those in Miami saw premiums skyrocket from $159,000 to more than $210,000. In states such as Pennsylvania, Nevada and Florida, doctors have retired early, left the state or stopped delivering babies to contain their insurance costs. While the overall number of doctors in these states is actually rising, certain specialties are feeling the pressure. Dr. Shripathi Holla, a neurosurgeon in Scranton, Pa., has seen his total malpractice insurance payments double in the last few years to approximately $150,000. Meanwhile, other area neurosurgeons have stopped practicing or retired early, and one recently moved to Maryland. "I am unable to recruit anyone to come to this town," says Holla. As a result, he finds himself on call for three different area hospitals on any given night, and he is sometimes the only surgeon willing to perform risky operations that trauma centers will no longer undertake. "Once some of us retire, this state is going to have a tremendous problem in terms of providing health care to its citizens," says Holla.

The Bush plan is modeled after California's 1975 Medical Injury Compensation Reform Act (MICRA). From 1976 to 2000, according to the AMA, California malpractice premiums remained stable, rising 167 percent compared with a 505 percent increase nationwide. However, California premiums increased dramatically in the years immediately following MICRA. They did not stabilize until 1988, three years after the California Supreme Court upheld MICRA and the same year that California voters passed Proposition 103, forcing publicly traded insurance companies to reduce rates by 20 percent. Both reforms likely played a role in stabilizing California's insurance rates.

The Importance of Deterrence

But critics of caps insist that pain and suffering damages are necessary to deter careless medical practice and compensate for injuries such as blindness, disfigurement and the loss of sex function, which cannot be quantified in economic terms. Limiting these awards, they argue, will do nothing to reduce costs to doctors and will only trample patients' rights. Linda McDougal, the Minnesota woman whose breasts were mistakenly removed after she was incorrectly diagnosed with cancer because her files were mixed up with another patient's, suffered few quantifiable economic losses. She had health insurance, and her employer covered medical bills and lost wages. But "she will have to go through life mutilated for no reason," says Carlton Carl of the Association of Trial Lawyers of America. George Annas of the Boston University School of Public Health contends that doctors in general are far too worried about being sued.

"Most doctors don't get sued," says Annas, referring to a 1990 Harvard study showing that only one in eight malpractice victims ever takes his or her case to court. "Compare that to patients who worry about being killed; it's not even in the same league."

Far more effective than an arbitrary cap on damages would be a more systematic effort to weed out bad doctors and prevent malpractice in the first place. Dr. Sidney Wolfe, director of Public Citizen's Health Research Group, says, "You should protect patients with doctor discipline and protect good doctors with low premiums." Public Citizen ranks state medical boards according to their records of disciplining negligent doctors. "Five percent of the doctors account for 50 percent of the malpractice payouts," he says. "The primary failing is at disciplining doctors. A lot could be remedied by taking bad doctors out of practice."

A Need for Insurance Reform

Meanwhile, CEO Richard Anderson and President Manuel Puebla of the Doctors' Company, a so-called physician-owned mutual, each earn approximately $2 million per year. Wolfe declares that doctors are "being used as a human shield by the malpractice insurance companies" who want tort reform to protect only themselves. After all, in many states where caps have been enacted, insurance premiums have continued to rise. Nevada, Missouri and Ohio all have some form of cap, but all three figure prominently on the AMA's "crisis states" map. Instead of turning their backs on the real causes, Wolfe says, doctors "should be marching for discipline reform and insurance reform."

Dr. Marcia Angell, former editor of *The New England Journal of Medicine* and now a professor at Harvard Medical School, is not surprised. "[Doctors] are not economists. They don't think in terms of how a business makes up for a loss of profits. They have been at loggerheads with the trial lawyers for so long that it's always a knee-jerk reaction." Moreover, she observes, many lawsuits arise due to the lack of a social safety net. "As long as we have a system based on avoiding sick people and not taking care of them, you leave sick and injured people with very little alternative other than to sue and to get some care that way," says Angell.

Remarkably enough, insurance companies don't even promise that a cap on lawsuits will solve the problem. In 2002, the American Insurance Association noted, "The insurance industry never promised that tort reform would achieve specific premium savings." And American Tort Reform Association President Sherman Joyce told *Liability Week* in 1999, "We wouldn't tell you or anyone that the reason to pass tort reform would be to reduce insurance rates." If doctors are genuinely concerned about reducing the cost of malpractice premiums and not simply shielding themselves from liability, it would only be logical to demand that for every dollar an insurance company saves as a result of tort reform, doctors should save a dollar on their premiums. . . .

AMA President-elect Dr. Donald Palmisano concedes that other remedies are available. In Massachusetts, Indiana and Louisiana, malpractice lawsuits undergo a pre-screening process, substantially reducing the number of questionable lawsuits without restricting the rights of patients to sue. Other top AMA officials admit that the caps for which they are lobbying hard may not even bring premiums down. "Dropping premiums would be great, but stabilizing is what we want," says an AMA spokeswoman. But stabilizing rates at levels that are already driving neurosurgeons and obstetricians out of business is no solution. While a cap on pain and suffering damages may result in marginal savings for general practitioners, there is no evidence that it would provide relief to those who perform the riskiest procedures. If the AMA succeeds in passing a $250,000 cap without a provision forcing insurance companies to pass their savings on to doctors, rates may well continue to climb, in which case growing numbers of obstetricians will stop delivering babies, more neurosurgeons will retire early or shy away from risky procedures, and more mutilated patients will be denied compensation.

> "[G]overnment intrusion in the health-
> care industry only makes health care
> less affordable and the quality of care
> lower."

Universal Health Care Will Reduce the Quality of American Medicine

Adam P. Summers

Universal health care will not improve medicine or reduce health-care costs, argues Adam P. Summers in the following viewpoint. Indeed, he maintains, government involvement in medical care has thus far increased costs and lowered the quality of care. Quality medical care requires that doctors and patients have control over medical decisions, Summers asserts. However, government-funded universal health care will turn medical decision making over to third-party bureaucrats, he claims. Summers is a policy analyst with the Reason Foundation, a Libertarian think tank.

As you read, consider the following questions:

1. What goals has government intrusion in the medical care industry failed to achieve, according to Summers?

2. What does Summers predict will be the outcome of California's universal healthcare plan?

3. In what way should medical care be like choosing an auto mechanic, in the author's opinion?

It seems everyone is jumping on board the health care reform bandwagon these days. President [George W.] Bush discussed his health care tax credit during his [2007] State of the Union address, [California] Gov. [Arnold] Schwarzenegger announced his statewide universal health care plan, and Democratic 2008 presidential candidates Hillary Clinton, Barack Obama, and Dennis Kucinich have all made nationwide universal health care a major plank in their campaign platforms.

Numerous others have decried sharply rising health care costs and offered many proposals, but no one can agree on a solution. One common thread to the proposed "solutions," however, is more government involvement, be it more taxes, more program expansions, more subsidies, or more mandates and regulations. Yet, government intrusion in the medical care industry has been increasing significantly for years—particularly since the birth of Medicare and Medicaid in 1965—without ever achieving the promised goals of greater affordability and better quality of care. It is no accident that the rising prices and declining quality of medical services coincide with an increasing socialization of the health care industry in America. Perhaps it is time to reexamine what it is we are trying to fix.

California's Plan

Gov. Schwarzenegger wants to enforce universal health care to cover 6.5 million uninsured Californians at an estimated cost of $12 billion a year. Remember: these are government cost estimates. Expect actual costs to be many times higher. The plan would require all of us to maintain at least a government-approved level of coverage—whether we want to or not—and

Making Health Care Worse

Universal health care will make care worse for almost everybody. Why should your company continue to pay for an excellent health care plan for retirees or current employees when the government does it for free? A company program that you liked could be replaced with a less personal and friendly system. The doctors you knew and trusted could be replaced overnight, disrupting your continuity of health care and treatment. Wage earners will see the value of their negotiated labor contracts fall in value with universal coverage, because part of the fringe benefits built into your total compensation paid for a superior health care plan.

Robert Meyer,
"Universal Health Care: An Idea Whose Time Should Never Come,"
Renew America, *March 20, 2007. www.renewamerica.us.*

would require insurers to issue policies to everyone, even those who wait to become sick before applying for "insurance." The plan would be paid for by a number of taxes, including a 2 percent tax on doctors and other medical professionals, a 4 percent tax on hospitals, and a 4 percent tax on employers with 10 or more workers that do not offer health benefits. Furthermore, the Schwarzenegger plan would increase eligibility requirements in the Healthy Families program to allow families with incomes of up to 300 percent of the poverty line (about $60,000 for a family of four) to obtain subsidized health insurance for children.

In short, California's universal health-care plan would (1) significantly increase insurance costs by artificially increasing demand and forcing the young and the healthy to compensate for the costs of the uninsurable who now must be covered; (2) increase the cost of services, as doctors and hospitals pass on the cost of higher taxes to their patients; (3) make employees less able to afford coverage, as employers respond to the tax increase by cutting salaries or dropping health-care coverage altogether, and (4) provide less incentive for families earning up to three times the poverty line to acquire private insurance, as more of them would be able to take advantage of the government dole.

Taking Away Patient Choice

One of the main problems with health care today is that medical decisions tend to be made by third-party bureaucrats— whether employees of the government or an HMO—rather than doctors and patients. Cost decisions, in particular, are completely taken away from the patient.

Last year [2006] I had to have a couple of radiological procedures done, and I had the audacity to ask the nurse in my doctor's office how much the procedure would cost. Not only could she not even give me a rough estimate, she looked at me as if this was the strangest thing I could have asked. Something is wrong with this picture. If I were to get into an auto accident or need some regular maintenance done on my car, there would be no question how much it would cost me. I could even go get several estimates and choose the best mechanic based on price and quality of work. Why should it be any different with medical care?

Voters are going to hear many health care "reform" proposals over the next couple of years (and beyond). The question they should ask themselves is: Does this plan give more power to me and my doctor or to third-party decision makers? The issue is freedom and control, and the one who pays is the one who controls.

After over a generation of taxes and mandates and regulations and Medicare, we can see that government intrusion in the health-care industry only makes health care less affordable and the quality of care lower. Politicians like Schwarzenegger, Clinton, Obama, and Ted Kennedy are right that the healthcare industry in our nation is sick. What they fail to realize is that government intervention is the disease, not the cure.

"*[W]hen you see what the health care crisis is doing to our families, to our economy, to our country, you realize that caution is what's costly.*"

Universal Health Care Is Necessary to Increase Access to Quality Medicine

Barack Obama

In the following viewpoint, U.S. Senator and 2008 presidential candidate Barack Obama argues that failing to develop a modern system of universal health coverage for all Americans poses a threat to American health. The cost of caring for the uninsured is passed on to American taxpayers, he maintains, and as premiums rise, more people, unable to afford health insurance, become uninsured, again increasing costs. In this vicious cycle, Obama claims, the number of uninsured Americans continues to grow. Adding to the problem, Obama asserts, is the money wasted on unnecessary paperwork that could be spent improving the quality of health care.

Barack Obama, "The Time Has Come for Universal Health Care," speech before the Families USA Conference, January 25, 2007. obama.senate.gov.

As you read, consider the following questions:

1. According to Obama, under what weight do most health care plans collapse after presidential campaigns end?
2. What statistics does the author cite to support his opinion that America's healthcare system is in crisis?
3. In the author's view, what will reduce the amount of money spent on bills and paperwork?

On this January morning of two thousand and seven, more than sixty years after President Truman first issued the call for national health insurance, we find ourselves in the midst of an historic moment on health care. From Maine to California, from business to labor, from Democrats to Republicans, the emergence of new and bold proposals from across the spectrum has effectively ended the debate over whether or not we should have universal health care in this country.

Plans that tinker and halfway measures now belong to yesterday. The President's [George W. Bush's] latest proposal that does little to bring down cost or guarantee coverage falls into this category. There will be many others offered in the coming campaign, and I am working with experts to develop my own plan as we speak, but let's make one thing clear right here, right now:

In the 2008 campaign, affordable, universal health care for every single American must not be a question of whether, it must be a question of how. We have the ideas, we have the resources, and we will have universal health care in this country by the end of the next president's first term.

A Reason for Cynicism

I know there's a cynicism out there about whether this can happen, and there's reason for it. Every four years, health care plans are offered up in campaigns with great fanfare and promise. But once those campaigns end, the plans collapse under the weight of Washington politics, leaving the rest of America to struggle with skyrocketing costs.

For too long, this debate has been stunted by what I call the smallness of our politics—the idea that there isn't much we can agree on or do about the major challenges facing our country. And when some try to propose something bold, the interest groups and the partisans treat it like a sporting event, with each side keeping score of who's up and who's down, using fear and divisiveness and other cheap tricks to win their argument, even if we lose our solution in the process.

Well we can't afford another disappointing charade in 2008. It's not only tiresome, it's wrong. Wrong when businesses have to layoff one employee because they can't afford the health care of another. Wrong when a parent cannot take a sick child to the doctor because they cannot afford the bill that comes with it. Wrong when 46 million Americans have no health care at all. In a country that spends more on health care than any other nation on Earth, it's just wrong.

Tinkering Not Enough

And yet, in recent years, what's caught the attention of those who haven't always been in favor of reform is the realization that this crisis isn't just morally offensive, it's economically untenable. For years, the can't-do crowd has scared the American people into believing that universal health care would mean socialized medicine and burdensome taxes—that we should just stay out of the way and tinker at the margins.

You know the statistics. Family premiums are up by nearly 87% over the last five years, growing five times faster than workers' wages. Deductibles are up 50%. Co-payments for care and prescriptions are through the roof.

Nearly 11 million Americans who are already insured spent more than a quarter of their salary on health care last year. And over half of all family bankruptcies today are caused by medical bills.

Should Government Guarantee Health Insurance for All?

Yes

64%

No

27%

Which Is More Serious?

Providing health insurance for all

65%

Keeping health care costs down

31%

TAKEN FROM: CBS News/*New York Times* poll, March 1, 2007.

Answering the Critics

But they say it's too costly to act.

Almost half of all small businesses no longer offer health care to their workers, and so many others have responded to rising costs by laying off workers or shutting their doors for good. Some of the biggest corporations in America, giants of industry like GM and Ford, are watching foreign competitors based in countries with universal health care run circles around them, with a GM car containing twice as much health care cost as a Japanese car.

But they say it's too risky to act.

They tell us it's too expensive to cover the uninsured, but they don't mention that every time an American without health insurance walks into an emergency room, we pay even more. Our family's premiums are $922 higher because of the cost of care for the uninsured.

We pay $15 billion more in taxes because of the cost of care for the uninsured. And it's trapped us in a vicious cycle.

As the uninsured cause premiums to rise, more employers drop coverage. As more employers drop coverage, more people become uninsured, and premiums rise even further.

But the skeptics tell us that reform is too costly, too risky, too impossible for America.

Well the skeptics must be living somewhere else. Because when you see what the health care crisis is doing to our families, to our economy, to our country, you realize that caution is what's costly. Inaction is what's risky. Doing nothing is what's impossible when it comes to health care in America.

It's time to act. This isn't a problem of money, this is a problem of will. A failure of leadership. We already spend $2.2 trillion a year on health care in this country. My colleague, Senator Ron Wyden, who's recently developed a bold new health care plan of his own, tells it this way:

> For the money Americans spent on health care last year, we could have hired a group of skilled physicians, paid each one of them $200,000 to care for just seven families, and guaranteed every single American quality, affordable health care.

Updating Technologies

So where's all that money going? We know that a quarter of it—one out of every four health care dollars—is spent on non-medical costs; mostly bills and paperwork. And we also know that this is completely unnecessary. Almost every other industry in the world has saved billions on these administrative costs by doing it all online. Every transaction you make at a bank now costs them less than a penny. Even at the Veterans Administration, where it used to cost nine dollars to pull up your medical record, new technology means you can call up the same record on the internet for next to nothing.

But because we haven't updated technology in the rest of the health care industry, a single transaction still costs up to twenty-five dollars—not one dime of which goes toward improving the quality of our health care.

This is simply inexcusable, and if we brought our entire health care system online, something everyone from Ted Kennedy to Newt Gingrich believes we should do, we'd already be saving over $600 million a year on health care costs.

The federal government should be leading the way here. If you do business with the federal employee health benefits program, you should move to an electronic claims system. If you are a provider who works with Medicare, you should have to report your patient's health outcomes, so that we can figure out, on a national level, how to improve health care quality. These are all things experts tell us must be done but aren't being done. And the federal government should lead. . . .

Shaping History

The debate in this country over health care has shifted. The support for comprehensive reform that organizations like Families USA have worked so hard to build is now widespread, and the diverse group of business and health industry interests that are part of your Health Care Coverage Coalition is a testament to that success. And so Washington no longer has an excuse for caution. Leaders no longer have a reason to be timid. And America can no longer afford inaction. That's not who we are—and that's not the story of our nation's improbable progress. . . .

Never forget that we have it within our power to shape history in this country. It is not in our character to sit idly by as victims of fate or circumstance, for we are a people of action and innovation, forever pushing the boundaries of what's possible.

Now is the time to push those boundaries once more. We have come so far in the debate on health care in this country, but now we must finally answer the call first issued by [former President Harry] Truman, advanced by [former President Lyndon] Johnson, and fought for by so many leaders and Americans throughout the last century. The time has come for universal health care in America. And I look forward to working with all of you to meet this challenge in the weeks and months to come.

> *"Stories of neglect and substandard care have flooded in from soldiers, their family members, veterans, doctors and nurses working inside the [military health care] system."*

Inadequate Medical Care Is a Serious Problem for U.S. Soldiers

Anne Hull and Dana Priest

Following a February 18, 2007, article exposing the mistreatment of wounded U.S. soldiers at Walter Reed Army Medical Center, U.S. soldiers flooded staff writers Anne Hull and Dana Priest with reports of substandard care nationwide. Many soldiers wait interminably in moldy, mice-ridden buildings, only to face a bureaucratic nightmare, the authors assert in the following viewpoint. Angry citizens and veterans are appalled and some embarrassed that they believed government assurances that wounded soldiers are being cared for, the authors claim. Now that the U.S. Congress is willing to criticize the Bush Administration, they reason, perhaps allegations of neglect will no longer fall on deaf ears.

As you read, consider the following questions:

1. What has been the official reaction to revelations of mistreatment at Walter Reed, according to Hull and Priest?

2. How have many outside Washington, D.C. communicated their concerns about allegations of mistreatment of U.S. soldiers at Walter Reed, in the authors' view?

3. In the authors' opinion, how long have politicians received letters from veterans complaining of poor care?

Ray Oliva went into the spare bedroom in his home in Kelseyville, Calif., to wrestle with his feelings. He didn't know a single soldier at Walter Reed, but he felt he knew them all. He worried about the wounded who were entering the world of military health care, which he knew all too well. His own VA [Veterans Administration] hospital in Livermore was a mess. The gown he wore was torn. The wheelchairs were old and broken.

"It is just not Walter Reed," Oliva slowly tapped out on his keyboard at 4:23 in the afternoon on Friday [March 2, 2007]. "The VA hospitals are not good either except for the staff who work so hard. It brings tears to my eyes when I see my brothers and sisters having to deal with these conditions. I am 70 years old, some say older than dirt but when I am with my brothers and sisters we become one and are made whole again."

Oliva is but one quaking voice in a vast outpouring of accounts filled with emotion and anger about the mistreatment of wounded outpatients at Walter Reed Army Medical Center. Stories of neglect and substandard care have flooded in from soldiers, their family members, veterans, doctors and nurses working inside the system. They describe depressing living conditions for outpatients at other military bases around the country, from Fort Lewis in Washington state to Fort Dix in New Jersey. They tell stories—their own versions, not verified—of callous responses to combat stress and a system ill equipped to handle another generation of psychologically scarred vets.

Reactions to the Scandal

The official reaction to the revelations at Walter Reed has been swift, and it has exposed the potential political costs of ignoring Oliva's 24.3 million comrades—America's veterans—many of whom are among the last standing supporters of the Iraq war. The Army secretary has been fired, a two-star general relieved of command and two special commissions appointed; congressional subcommittees are lining up for hearings, the first [on March 5, 2007] at Walter Reed; and the president, in his weekly radio address, redoubled promises to do right by the all-volunteer force, 1.5 million of whom have fought in Iraq and Afghanistan.

But much deeper has been the reaction outside Washington, including from many of the 600,000 new veterans who left the service after Iraq and Afghanistan. Wrenching questions have dominated blogs, talk shows, editorial cartoons, VFW [Veterans of Foreign Wars] spaghetti suppers and the solitary late nights of soldiers and former soldiers who fire off e-mails to reporters, members of Congress and the White House—looking, finally, for attention and solutions.

Several forces converged to create this intense reaction. A new Democratic majority in Congress is willing to criticize the administration. Senior retired officers pounded the Pentagon with sharp questions about what was going on. Up to 40 percent of the troops fighting in Iraq are National Guard members and reservists—"our neighbors," said Ron Glasser, a physician and author of a book about the wounded. "It all adds up and reaches a kind of tipping point," he said. On top of all that, America had believed the government's assurances that the wounded were being taken care of. "The country is embarrassed" to know otherwise, Glasser said.

The scandal has reverberated through generations of veterans. "It's been a potent reminder of past indignities and past traumas," said Thomas A. Mellman, a professor of psychiatry at Howard University who specializes in post-traumatic stress and has worked in Veterans Affairs hospitals. "The fact that it's been responded to so quickly has created mixed feelings—gratification, but obvious regret and anger that such attention wasn't given before, especially for Vietnam veterans."

Across the country, some military quarters for wounded outpatients are in bad shape, according to interviews, Government Accountability Office reports and transcripts of congressional testimony. The mold, mice and rot of Walter Reed's Building 18 compose a familiar scenario for many soldiers back from Iraq or Afghanistan who were shipped to their home posts for treatment. Nearly 4,000 outpatients are currently in the military's Medical Holding or Medical Holdover companies, which oversee the wounded. Soldiers and veterans report bureaucratic disarray similar to Walter Reed's: indifferent, untrained staff; lost paperwork; medical appointments that drop from the computer; and long waits for consultations.

Telling Their Stories

Sandy Karen was horrified when her 21-year-old son was discharged from the Naval Medical Center in San Diego a few months ago and told to report to the outpatient barracks, only to find the room swarming with fruit flies, trash overflowing and a syringe on the table. "The staff sergeant says, 'Here are your linens' to my son, who can't even stand up," said Karen, of Brookeville, Md. "This kid has an open wound, and I'm going to put him in a room with fruit flies?" She took her son to a hotel instead.

"My concern is for the others, who don't have a parent or someone to fight for them," Karen said. "These are just kids. Who would have ever looked in on my son?"

Capt. Leslie Haines was sent to Fort Knox in Kentucky for treatment in 2004 after being flown out of Iraq. "The living conditions were the worst I'd ever seen for soldiers," he said. "Paint peeling, mold, windows that didn't work. I went to the hospital chaplain to get them to issue blankets and linens. There were no nurses. You had wounded and injured leading the troops."

Hundreds of soldiers contacted *The Washington Post* through telephone calls and e-mails, many of them describing their bleak existence in Medhold.

From Fort Campbell in Kentucky: "There were yellow signs on the door stating our barracks had asbestos."

From Fort Bragg in North Carolina: "They are on my [expletive] like a diaper . . . there are people getting chewed up everyday."

From Fort Dix in New Jersey: "Scare tactics are used against soldiers who will write sworn statement to assist fellow soldiers for their medical needs."

From Fort Irwin in California: "Most of us have had to sign waivers where we understand that the housing we were in failed to meet minimal government standards."

Soldiers back from Iraq worry that their psychological problems are only beginning to surface. "The hammer is just coming down, I can feel it," said retired Maj. Anthony DeStefano of New Jersey, describing his descent into post-traumatic stress and the Army's propensity to medicate rather than talk. When he returned home, Army doctors put him on the antipsychotic drug Seroquel. "That way, you can screw their lights out and they won't feel a thing," he said of patients like himself. "By the time they understand what is going on, they are through the Board and stuck with an unfavorable percentage of disability" benefits.

Nearly 64,000 of the more than 184,000 Iraq and Afghanistan war veterans who have sought VA health care have been diagnosed with potential symptoms of post-traumatic stress, drug abuse or other mental disorders as of the end of June, according to the latest report by the Veterans Health Administration. Of those, nearly 30,000 have possible post-traumatic stress disorder, the report said.

A Surge of Patients

VA hospitals are also receiving a surge of new patients after more than five years of combat. At the sprawling James J. Peters VA Medical Center in the Bronx, N.Y., Spec. Roberto Reyes Jr. lies nearly immobile and unable to talk. Once a strapping member of Charlie Company, 1st Battalion, 5th Cavalry, Reyes got too close to an improvised explosive device in Iraq and was sent to Walter Reed, where doctors did all they could before shipping him to the VA for the remainder of his life. A cloudy bag of urine hangs from his wheelchair. His mother and his aunt are constant bedside companions; Reyes, 25, likes for them to get two inches from his face, so he can pull on their noses with the few fingers he can still control.

Maria Mendez, his aunt, complained about the hospital staff. "They fight over who's going to have to give him a bath—in front of him!" she said. Reyes suffered third-degree burns on his leg when a nurse left him in a shower unattended. He was unable to move himself away from the scalding water. His aunt found out only later, when she saw the burns.

An Open Secret

Among the most aggrieved are veterans who have lived with the open secret of substandard, underfunded care in the 154 VA hospitals and hundreds of community health centers around the country. They vented their fury in thousands of e-mails and phone calls and in chat rooms.

"I have been trying to get someone, ANYBODY, to look into my allegations" at the Dayton VA, pleaded Darrell Hampton.

"I'm calling from Summerville, South Carolina, and I have a story to tell," began Horace Williams, 62. "I'm a Marine from the Vietnam era, and it took me 20 years to get the benefits I was entitled to."

The VA has a backlog of 400,000 benefit claims, including many concerning mental health. Vietnam vets whose post-traumatic stress has been triggered by images of war in Iraq are flooding the system for help and are being turned away.

For years, politicians have received letters from veterans complaining of bad care across the country. Last week, Walter Reed was besieged by members of Congress who toured the hospital and Building 18 to gain first-hand knowledge of the conditions. Many of them have been visiting patients in the hospital for years, but now they are issuing news releases decrying the mistreatment of the wounded.

Sgt. William A. Jones had recently written to his Arizona senators complaining about abuse at the VA hospital in Phoenix. He had written to the president before that. "Not one person has taken the time to respond in any manner," Jones said in an e-mail.

From Ray Oliva, the distraught 70-year-old vet from Kelseyville, Calif., came this: "I wrote a letter to Senators Feinstein and Boxer a few years ago asking why I had to wear Hospital gowns that had holes in them and torn and why some of the Vets had to ask for beds that had good mattress instead of broken and old. Wheel chairs old and tired and the list goes on and on. I never did get a response."

Oliva lives in a house on a tranquil lake. His hearing is shot from working on fighter jets on the flight line. "Gun plumbers," as they called themselves, didn't get earplugs in the late 1950s, when Oliva served with the Air Force. His hands had been burned from touching the skin of the aircraft. All is minor compared with what he later saw at the VA hospital where he received care.

"I sat with guys who'd served in 'Nam," Oliva said. "We had terrible problems with the VA. But we were all so powerless to do anything about them. Just like Walter Reed."

I *"Wars are unpredictable, and military*
medical systems often struggle to cope."

War's Unpredictability Explains the Challenges Faced by U.S. Military Medical Care

Economist

Claims that the U.S. government has deliberately neglected its wounded soldiers in order to reduce costs are unfair and simplistic, claim the editors of the Economist *in the following viewpoint. Wars often bring surprises that can overwhelm military health-care systems, they assert. The war in Iraq has lasted longer than expected and more soldiers have survived their injuries. As a result, the authors reason, a greater number of wounded soldiers need care. The crucial question is whether the military health-care system will learn the lessons of the Iraq war as it has learned from past wars, the British news magazine's editors conclude.*

"Broken Reed; The Military Health-Care Scandal," *The Economist*, vol. 382, March 10, 2007, p. 29. Copyright © 2007 Economist Newspaper Ltd. Republished with permission of *The Economist*, conveyed through Copyright Clearance Center, Inc.

As you read, consider the following questions:

1. According to the *Economist*, what percentage of soldiers needing amputations after serving in Iraq and Afghanistan have been treated at Walter Reed Army Medical Center?

2. In the authors' opinion, how have politicians of both parties used the scandal to "score points" on issues that concern them?

3. What U.S. military health care reforms have come as a result of past wars, in the authors' view?

Inside the steel fence that surrounds the Walter Reed Army Medical Centre are some grisly sights. A pile of amputated limbs sits glistening in the sunlight. Surgeons prepare to operate with unwashed hands and filthy instruments, virtually ensuring infection. These are not scenes from the hospital itself, of course, but exhibits in the museum of military medicine in its grounds. Visitors are reminded that the . . . scandal over conditions at Walter Reed is hardly unprecedented.

Walter Reed is America's foremost military hospital. Nearly four-fifths of the soldiers who have needed amputations after serving in Iraq or Afghanistan have been treated there. The surgery they receive is, by all accounts, superb. But the bureaucracy that engulfs them afterwards is not.

Last month [February 2007] the *Washington Post* published an exposé. It described a building housing outpatients: "Signs of neglect are everywhere: mouse droppings, belly-up cockroaches, stained carpets, cheap mattresses." Wounded soldiers needing to get their papers processed, so they could return either to active duty or civilian life, faced 16 different information systems, few able to communicate with each other. One amputee received orders to report to a base in Germany "as he sat drooling in his wheelchair in a haze of medication."

A System Overwhelmed

On Monday, [March 5, 2007] the Army's inspector general issued a report concluding that the thousands of soldiers wounded in Iraq and Afghanistan have overwhelmed the Army's system for determining eligibility for disability benefits. The vast majority of these reviews drag on long after Army standards say they should be completed. . . .

As a result, thousands of wounded soldiers are left in the dark as to whether or not their military careers are over, making it impossible for them to move on with their lives. . . .

Many of them praised the direct medical care provided by Walter Reed and paid tribute to the dedication of the doctors, nurses and case workers. It was the system, many said, that was broken and unresponsive to their needs.

Barry Grey, "Government Indifference,
Cost-Cutting Compound Ravages of War for Wounded U.S. Troops,"
World Socialist Web Site, *March 15, 2007. www.wsws.org.*

The report sparked outrage. Both George Weightman, the head of Walter Reed, and Francis Harvey, the secretary of the army, were sacked. Both arms of Congress held hearings. On March 5th [2007] the House oversight committee heard testimony from John Shannon, an infantry sergeant who was shot in the head near the Saddam Mosque in Ramadi, [Iraq] causing brain trauma and the loss of an eye. Wearing a patch over the empty socket, Sergeant Shannon told how he was discharged from a ward at Walter Reed and told to make his own way to an outpatient building while utterly disorientated. He spoke of a bureaucracy so inept that his case manager could not find him for several weeks, although he was sitting in the outpatient room where he had been sent. He said he had seen "many soldiers get so frustrated with the process that they will sign anything presented [to] them just so they can get on with their lives." He suggested that this was how the government reduced the cost of caring for veterans.

President George Bush promised action. He has appointed a bipartisan commission to investigate the military health-care system, to be headed by Bob Dole, a former Republican presidential nominee and veteran of the second world war, and Donna Shalala, who was health secretary under [former President] Bill Clinton. Meanwhile, politicians of both parties sought to score points. "This is the Katrina of 2007," said Chuck Schumer, a Democratic senator, evoking the government's poor response to the hurricane that flooded New Orleans in 2005. Conservatives pointed to Walter Reed as a sign of what government-controlled health care would be like.

The truth is more complicated. Wars are unpredictable, and military medical systems often struggle to cope. Among the surprises thrown up by the Iraq war, two have aggravated the problems at Walter Reed. First, the war has lasted much longer than expected. Second, American body armour and battlefield medicine are now so good that some 90% of wounded soldiers survive. In Vietnam, the figure was 76%. During the American civil war [1861–1865], most soldiers with injuries died of them.

Both factors have contributed to a higher-than-expected tally of wounded Americans—24,000 so far in Iraq and Afghanistan [as of March 2007]. Many of these need long-term care. Many suffer lost limbs or mental problems. Their armoured cars and Kevlar vests prevent the shrapnel from roadside bombs from killing them, but the blast still buffets their brains. Two-thirds of all injuries are from bombs, and of these some 28% involve brain trauma, according to the Department of Defence.

Lack of money is not the problem. The Department of Defence's health budget has grown from $19 billion a year to

$38 billion under Mr Bush. The Veterans Administration, which provides health care for veterans who lack insurance, spends nearly as much. Both systems have their strengths, says Daniel Johnson, a former military doctor and now health-policy analyst at the Heritage Foundation, a conservative think-tank. But their computers cannot speak to each other, and they offer far less choice than, for example, the much-admired health plan for civilian federal employees. He says he hopes the scandal will spur overdue reforms.

In past conflicts that has often happened. During the civil war, the scandal of wounded soldiers left lying for days on the battlefield prompted the creation of an efficient evacuation system. The second world war spurred the mass-production of penicillin. In 2002 the army introduced high-tech bandages with coagulants to stop wounds bleeding. Walter Reed itself does sterling research into telemedicine and vaccines. The question is, can it also learn to do the boring stuff well?

Periodical Bibliography

The following articles have been selected to supplement the diverse views presented in this chapter.

Scott W. Atlas	"Tear Down Those Health-Care Walls," *Washington Times*, March 9, 2007.
Ronald Bailey	"2005 Medical Care Forever," *Reason*, June 15, 2005.
Roger G. Beauchamp	"Commentary: Restoring Individual Rights and Health Care Freedom," *Health Care News*, April 2007.
Randall R. Bovbjerg and Randolph W. Pate	"How Should Malpractice Policy Put Patients First?" *AARP Bulletin*, April 2006
Lance Dickie	"Opinion: Why the Nation Will Embrace Universal Health Care," *Seattle Times*, June 3, 2005.
Miguel A. Faria	"Medical Liability Tort Reform: A Neurosurgeon's Perspective," *Surgical Neurology*, March 2004.
Martin Frazier	"Health Care Racism Kills 83,000 Yearly," *People's Weekly World*, March 31, 2005.
William H. Frist	"Overcoming Disparities in U.S. Health Care," *Health Affairs*, March/April 2005.
Timothy Johnson	"Universal Health Care: We Can't Afford Not To," *USA Today*, October 19, 2006.
Kenneth Jost	"Medical Malpractice," *CQ Researcher*, February 14, 2003.
New Republic	"Moral Imperative," March 20–June 5, 2006.
Doug Pibel and Sarah van Gelder	"Health Care: It's What Ails Us," *Yes! Magazine*, Fall 2006.
Lorraine Woellert	"Commentary: A Second Opinion on the Malpractice Plague," *Business Week*, March 3, 2003.

CHAPTER 2

OPPOSING
VIEWPOINTS®
SERIES

Is Alternative
Medicine Effective?

Chapter Preface

More than thirty thousand different dietary supplements are available in the United States. Millions of Americans spend nearly $16 billion each year on these supplements, which range from herbals, botanicals, and vitamins and minerals to amino acids, enzymes, and metabolites. While immensely popular, little is known about the long-term effects of these dietary supplements. The weight loss and energy supplement ephedra was linked to more than 150 deaths before it was banned in the spring of 2004. Ephedra had been on the market for many years before reports of its health risks began to surface.

Due in large part to American's growing acceptance of non-traditional, alternative medicine, Congress passed the Dietary Supplement Health and Education Act (DSHEA) in 1994, which left the supplement industry largely unregulated. Unlike prescription and over-the-counter drugs, federal oversight of supplements is similar to that of food: they are presumed safe unless the Food and Drug Administration (FDA) proves otherwise. Charles Bell of the Consumers Union reports, however, that in 2002 the American Association of Poison Control Centers received 22,928 reports of bad reactions involving herbal and homeopathic dietary supplements. Of those reactions, nearly 40 percent required medical treatment. One of several questions in the debate over the effectiveness of alternative medicine is whether these increasingly popular dietary supplements are indeed dangerous substances in need of regulation.

Industry advocates oppose increasing federal oversight, arguing that supplements are comparatively safe. David Seckman, executive director of National Nutritional Foods Association (NNFA) maintains that, compared to prescription medication or food-borne illnesses, "supplements are actually very safe." Seckman claims that more than 5,000 Americans are killed each year by food-borne illness, 17,000 from pain relievers such as ibuprofen, and 106,000 from prescription drugs. Supplement supporters maintain that costly oversight is unnecessary when self-regulation has, overall, been effective. The media, they argue, has blown the risks of some supplements out of proportion, unfairly blaming the entire industry for the unethical practices of a few. "DSHEA already allows for the necessary oversight of dietary supplements," Seckman reasons, "and doesn't need to be changed."

Critics counter that industry oversight is not enough. Metabolife, for example, continued to market its dietary supplement despite having received nearly fifteen thousand reports of adverse reactions over five years. The company was ultimately indicted for lying to the FDA. Moreover, critics claim, unsafe prescription and over-the-counter drugs can be removed from the market more quickly than supplements because drugs are subject to stricter rules. The diet drug fen-phen, critics point out, was removed within three months of learning it was merely *suspected* in thirty-three cases of a rare heart disease. It took 105 deaths over ten years, however, before the FDA had ephedra taken off the market because the FDA had to prove the supplement's dangers—a long, arduous process. "It is shocking . . . that dietary supplements are now subject to lower safety standards than are food additives and that consumers are provided with more information about the composition and nutritional value of a loaf of bread than about the ingredients and potential hazards of botanical medicines," says State University of New York pharmacology professor Arthur Grollman.

To strengthen oversight of dietary supplements, U.S. Representative Dan Burton (R-IN) introduced the DSHEA Full Implementation and Enforcement Act of 2007, on June 14 of that year. As of this writing, the bill remains in committee where the debate over the dangers of supplements continues.

The authors in the following chapter explore other controversies in the debate over the effectiveness of alternative therapies.

"The trouble is that many alternative therapies are based on unscientific, essentially magical thinking, and the proponents of these therapies, such as homeopathy, claim that they cannot be tested scientifically, effectively barricading them from criticism."

Alternative Medicine Is Dangerous and Scientifically Unproven

Clare Bowerman

In the following viewpoint, journalist Clare Bowerman claims that many of the alternative treatments that she herself touted as an alternative health journalist have not been scientifically proven to be safe or effective. Print journalists may appear to present a balanced view of alternative medicine, she asserts, but for many readers a personal success story about alternative therapy is more appealing than dry statistics reporting its dangers. Rather than make alternative medicine appear glamorous, Bowerman argues, journalists should inform the public that claims of alternative medicine remain unproven. Bowerman currently writes about evidence-based medicine.

Clare Bowerman, "Confessions of a Former Alternative Health Journalist," *Skeptic*, vol. 11, summer 2004, pp. 60–65. Copyright © 2004 Skeptics Society & *Skeptic* Magazine. Reproduced by permission.

As you read, consider the following questions:

1. What did Bowerman realize about her job when she learned that one of her readers sought only alternative medicine for a serious illness?

2. In evidence-based medicine, what medicines are alternative, in the author's view?

3. In the author's opinion, what privileged and dangerous position are journalists in?

- Alternative medicine is effective and benign.

- Alternative medicine is "natural," so it must be good for you.

- Alternative medicine can often cure disease when conventional medicine fails.

- Doctors are keeping the benefits of alternative medicine from the public.

- You can challenge the *status quo* of "mainstream" medicine simply by going for a massage, or taking herbal supplements.

These were the sort of messages we promoted when I was employed as an alternative health journalist. I worked for several years for a glossy magazine that supported and fed on the booming market for alternative medicines in the UK [United Kingdom]. I wrote stories on how St. John's Wort could cure depression, how being stroked with magnets could get rid of migraine headaches, and how taking supplements could cut your risk of cancer—all based on rehashed press releases from "scientific" trials of dubious quality. I didn't give an opposing opinion because such intellectual balance isn't the style for sleek women's magazines. . . .

A Castle in the Air

Then one day, things changed. A reader of the magazine called the editorial desk to ask for advice. A few years before, she told me, her daughter Anna had been afflicted with a mysterious illness. Anna had started to feel constantly ill and to lose weight. After a brief initial visit to her physician. Anna had opted for an alternative practitioner—a Chinese herbalist—who claimed she had "systemic" candida, an alleged condition in which a fungal infection affects the whole body. Mainstream practitioners regard the diagnosis with suspicion because generally, candida is considered to be a localized infection only. The herbalist had put Anna on a severely restricted diet that cut out any "yeast-forming" foods and had given her a concoction of herbs to take.

Several years after her first visit to the herbalist, the mother told me that Anna was still being treated unconventionally, and that they had foregone any mainstream medical care. She was still losing weight, now barely moving the scale at under a hundred pounds. She was in constant pain and had apparently had no romantic life in years.

During the conversation it dawned on me that my vague rationalizations about "perspective" were nonsense. I told Anna's mother that she needed to persuade her daughter to go back to her physician to ask for specialist tests, exactly as I would have done had I been in her place. The castle in the air came tumbling down.

Misinforming Readers

My experience with Anna was one of the main reasons I decided to leave the alternative medicine media and get into evidence-based medicine (EBM) media. I realized that with all of its glitz, glamour, and fairy dust, I wasn't taking my job seriously enough. When you are writing, you are often divorced from those you are writing for, and the consequences of what you say are lost. You spend your time pleasing the editor, and you forget the real needs of your readership. But health is a serious subject.

I've thought a lot about Anna since then. She could well have had a serious physical or mental illness. Because of her reliance on unproven medicines, it could have been getting worse for years. Perhaps Anna was a bit gullible. But it seems to me, in guilty retrospect, that journalists like me had misinformed her.

It isn't just glossy magazines that give an unbalanced view of alternative medicines. Books and newspapers often do the same, running pieces on these medicines without giving a balanced appraisal of their benefits and risks, or explaining how they contradict a scientific worldview.

What Is Alternative Medicine, Anyway?

One of the reasons that there is so much woolly writing about alternative medicine is that the term itself is woolly. It sounds glamorous, but what does it actually mean?

The Cochrane Collaboration, an organization that provides systematic reviews of controlled trials, uses the following definition:

> Complementary and alternative medicine [CAM] is a broad domain of healing resources that encompasses all health systems, modalities, and practices and their accompanying theories and beliefs, other than those intrinsic to the politically dominant health system of a particular society or culture in a given historical period. CAM includes all such practices and ideas self-defined by their users as preventing or treating illness or promoting health and well-being. Boundaries within CAM and between the CAM domain and that of the dominant (conventional) system are not always sharp or fixed.

This explanation is all very well, but it doesn't emphasize what our "politically dominant system" actually *is*. Not so

Alternative Medicine Is a Misnomer

There is really no such thing as alternative medicine. There can be alternatives in medicine (penicillin v. erythromycin) but there is no valid alternative to medicine. Either a treatment works, or it does not. As soon as science shows that a treatment works, it becomes a part of scientific medicine and is no longer considered "alternative."

Harriet Hall, "The Skep Doc: Keeping an Eye on Alternative Medicine," Skeptic, Winter 2006, pp. 25–26.

many years ago, a great deal of the "conventional" medicine meted out by doctors had no more basis in best evidence than alternative medicine has today. In fact, estimates in the early 1980s suggested that only 10–20% of medical interventions (such as drug therapies, blood tests, X-rays, and surgical operations) were based on sound scientific evidence. Critics of alternative medicine should not forget that there is still plenty of room for unscientific practice in the mainstream.

However, despite these flaws, evidence-based medicine [EBM] has been a driving force of the so-called "dominant system" for years. By its very nature, EBM is not an "establishment" but a principle that welcomes the changes driven by new evidence. If an herb is properly tested and shown to be a more effective and safe treatment than a pharmaceutical drug, then EBM would accept and prescribe it.

Because an evidence-based approach can absorb any type of treatment that has been shown to work according to a scientific method, the only medicines that are alternative to it are those that resist scientific analysis. . . .

Unproven Alternatives

The trouble is that many alternative therapies are based on unscientific, essentially magical thinking, and the proponents of these therapies, such as homeopathy, claim that they cannot be tested scientifically, effectively barricading them from criticism. And where trials have been conducted into homeopathy, for example, trial quality has been poor and results wanting.

But the message clearly isn't getting across. Unproven alternative therapies are more popular than ever: 69% of Americans use unconventional medical therapies, and 56% of Americans surveyed believe their health plans should cover alternative therapies. In one study, 50% of physicians surveyed expect to begin or increase usage of homeopathic and holistic recommendations over the next year. Patient acceptance is greater for these therapies, resulting in better compliance.

Would all of these people be so eager to try alternative treatments if they looked a little closer, and saw how many of these treatments are unproven, untested, potentially unsafe and probably unbeneficial? If a treatment can prove its worth in scientific trials, then it merits being backed by health insurers. If not, then we should strip away the dazzle. There is no reason that physicians should recommend an unproven medicine, insurers back it, or journalists promote it as a safe and natural alternative. . . .

Health in the News

It isn't just the shiny magazines that give unproven medicines such an easy ride. What is the attraction of unproven medicines for the weightier news publications, which wouldn't *dream* of being tied to the ad man?

Well, for a start, journalists need to make their work interesting and entertaining—otherwise nobody will read it. Even editorials in medical journals need to find a new and different angle, which often means discussing scare stories rather than genuine public health risks, and bizarre therapies rather than proven cures. Physician-turned-journalist Graham Easton clarified the dilemma of medical integrity and entertainment in a *British Medical Journal* editorial: "Reporting Risk: That's Entertainment."

Surprising angles, new scoops, wonder cures and personal accounts are all a lot more interesting to most readers than a bunch of hard statistics, and unproven remedies tend to be strong on personal anecdotes (and, of course, the one thing that unproven remedies *can't* provide is decent data!)

Journalists also need to give more than one opinion. In many health features and interviews, unproven alternative therapy can often seem like the perfect antidote to a dry medical expert. "Traditional" therapies versus "modern medicine," or "natural" versus "pharmaceutical," or "herbal" versus "drug"—the contrasts make for a compelling feature story.

But the trouble is, the two "sides" may not be as equal as they seem. Usually the "dry medical experts" will be talking from a far greater pool of knowledge, and they will have already weighed their reply according to the balance of evidence. Yet medical evidence may be far less persuasive than a personal story. . . .

Missing the Scientific Argument

Better investigative features do more than hang an argument between opposing views. They consider the ordering of these views carefully, and seek to position and frame information so that readers can understand the merit of each viewpoint. But even well-written features tend to miss the scientific argument. Take the case of St. John's Wort. This is considered to be the best researched of herbal remedies. In 1996, a review of trials on the herb was published in the *British Medical Journal*, which showed that the herb was as effective as antidepressants for mild to moderate depression, with few reported side-effects.

The story was eagerly taken up by the press. Features written at the time balanced the risks and benefits of standard antidepressants with the herb, and some mentioned the limitations of the St. John's Wort trials.

But very few press reports on St. John's Wort explained the general concerns that scientists had about herbal medicines. Reports did not explain, for example, that the herb had not been approved for use by the FDA. They also didn't mention that the use of herbs violates a principle of modern pharmacology which aims to isolate and understand the active ingredient in a curative substance for development into a drug.

This would have been highly relevant information in the case of St. John's Wort. Despite its success in trials, there was little understanding of what in the herb was having an effect, and how much of it was needed to work (trials showed a 17-fold difference between the quantities of hypericin found in different brands of St. John's Wort extract!). Although the herb seemed to have few side-effects, understanding of this treatment was much sketchier than it seemed.

Subsequently, it has emerged that St. John's Wort interacts with many prescription medicines, either preventing them from working or severely attenuating their effectiveness. Drugs that are affected by St. John's Wort include the contraceptive pill, the anticoagulant warfarin, and HIV protease inhibitors, including indinavir.

The late discovery of these interactions is intimately bound up with the vagueness around the research, control, and administration of herbal remedies. Had press reports covering St. John's Wort given more detail about these issues, it might have been clearer that the herb is not a safe alternative to antidepressants. . . .

Striving for Balance

It is easy to dismiss the acceptance of unproven medicines as consumer gullibility. But while you'd have to be pretty credulous to believe in some of the quackery out there, other health hoaxes are harder to detect.

Journalists and writers are in the privileged and dangerous position of influencing what people think and how they behave. All too often, health writing is about deadlines, the scoop, and the personal angle. But unless health writers dig beneath the surface of fashionable alternative medicines, unless we strive for true balance and scientific accuracy, people will continue to be misled. And they will continue to stake their hope and health on unproven and even dangerous cures.

"*[Alternative] treatments have proved to work just as well as modern medications—and in some cases even better.*"

Alternative Medicine Is Effective to Relieve Pain

Kristin Kane and Sharon Liao

In this viewpoint, authors Kristin Kane and Sharon Liao argue that, while many people rely on conventional, modern medications and procedures to help ease aches and pains, those people are missing out on "pain-defying alternatives." For common yet significant ailments such as headaches, sore throats, and joint and muscle pains, alternative treatments such as herbs and acupuncture have proved to work just as well as modern medicines. In some cases, say Kane and Liao, these healthy alternatives have worked even better than conventional methods. Kristin Kane is an associate editor with Prevention, *a healthy lifestyle magazine. Sharon Liao is a former associate editor with* Prevention.

As you read, consider the following questions:

1. How have healers treated migraines since the 17th Century, and how does this alternative treatment work?

2. Instead of purchasing expensive custom-made orthotics, what do foot experts suggest for heel pain?

3. What types of exercise have studies shown to help ease back pain?

Most of us have an old standby—aspirin, say—that we take for nearly everything that ails us. And it would seem we reach for it often: In any given 2-week stretch, more than half of American adults experience significant aches and pains, according to a study published in *JAMA* [*The Journal of the American Medical Association*]. If your approach has been limited to the same tired trick, you're missing out on decades of good research on pain-defying alternatives, such as herbs, acupuncture, and visualization. In studies, these [alternative] treatments have proved to work just as well as modern medications—and in some cases even better.

Whether it's a splitting headache, an aching neck, stiff joints, or a sprained ankle, we've found a natural fix for what ails you. Just make sure that you keep your doctor informed about any treatments you try.

Beat Migraines

Since the 17th century, healers have treated migraines with the herb butterbur (*Petasites hybridus* root). When German and American researchers tested it recently on 58 migraine sufferers—who took 75 mg of butterbur or a placebo twice a day for 4 months—the herb takers had migraines about half as often, compared with a 26% drop for the placebo takers.

Butterbur contains compounds that prevent blood vessel inflammation, a possible migraine trigger. If your migraines subside after 3 to 6 months of taking the herb, you can discontinue use (though you may need to restart treatment if the headaches return). . . .

Ease Headaches

Picture pleasant, tension-reducing images such as ocean waves, or visualize your pain as an object you can manipulate and banish from your body. That's how visualization—aka guided imagery—can help keep headaches at bay. (A therapist can lead you through the technique, but you can try it at home, too.)

In a monthlong study of 260 chronic tension-headache sufferers, about 22% of those who listened to guided imagery tapes 20 minutes a day reported that their aches were "much better" than before the treatment, compared with only 8% of the control group. . . .

Tame Tennis Elbow

Acupuncture is a miracle worker: When Mayo Clinic researchers gave 22 people with persistent tennis elbow four treatments with needles, 80% got complete and long-lasting relief; another 10% reported much less pain and improved mobility. "These patients had suffered for more than a year and had tried drugs, cortisone injections, wearing a brace, and even surgery," says study author Peter T. Dorsher, MD. "Acupuncture was the first intervention that worked for most of these patients."

Wipe out Wrist Pain

Whether you're suffering from an inflamed tendon or carpal tunnel syndrome (caused by swelling of the tissue around the medial nerve, which runs from your hand to forearm), restricting the motion of your wrist could be the answer. Try a splint that prevents your wrist from bending as you sleep, says Robert Werner, MD, a professor of physical medicine and rehabilitation at the University of Michigan. He asked 112 assembly line autoworkers with wrist pain to watch an ergonomic training video, then one group was told to wear a wrist splint at night; the other half went without.

After a month, reports of pain and numbness in the splint group fell by half; symptoms in the other group, by a quarter. The improvement lasted for up to a year. Get the ergonomic training if you can, but try the brace too: Choose a rigid one that keeps your hand in line with your forearm, Werner says. . . . Wear it while sleeping every night for about 6 weeks or until pain subsides.

Soothe a Sore Throat

A combo of marshmallow and licorice roots and slippery elm bark calms sore throats by protectively coating irritated membranes, reports a study published in the *Journal of Alternative and Complementary Medicine.* Sixty adults with inflamed throats drank either a tea containing these herbs or a placebo beverage four to six times a day for about a week.

Those who downed the brew reported 48% less pain than the placebo group. Throat Coat, the tea used in the study, is available online and in health food stores. Some people are sensitive to the herbs in the mix; if you have allergies or high blood pressure, check with your doc before steeping a mugful.

Calm Eczema

An immune system malfunction triggers eczema's dry, itchy rashes as white blood cells release substances that attack skin cells. Cortico-steroids can quell the white blood cells' reaction, but they may also irritate skin and, if used long-term, even cause bone loss. An alternative: B12 cream. In a 2-month multicenter study, German researchers asked 49 volunteers to put the cream on rashes on one side of their body and a placebo cream on the other.

Nearly 60% said the B12 cream relieved symptoms—the placebo helped only 11%. Researchers say topical vitamin B12 inhibits the faulty immune response; the cream should be available in the United States later this year. Or you could ask a compounding pharmacist to mix up a cream at 0.07% strength. . . .

Pacify Inflamed Joints

A mix of plant and tree bark extracts reduces joint pain just as well as NSAIDs such as Vioxx, found University of Exeter, UK, scientists. They looked at studies involving a total of 820 patients who took either the herb blend, called Phytodolor, or an NSAID three times a day for 2 to 4 weeks. Those who got Phytodolor not only felt as much relief as people taking NSAIDs, they also experienced fewer side effects such as stomach pain and dizziness. German researchers who compared the herb blend to aspirin found that Phytodolor was twice as effective at suppressing enzymes that induce arthritis swelling and pain. . . .

A better-known duo, glucosamine and chondroitin, has yet to convince researchers. It seems to help moderate joint pain but does little for severe cases. There is one other option: Studies on capsaicin suggest that this compound—found in chile peppers—helps relieve pain by interfering with a chemical that tells your brain you're hurting. . . .

Save a Sprained Ankle

Hobble to your local pharmacy or health food store and pick up a tube of comfrey ointment. This weed, which grows in marshes, is high in allantoin, a substance that reduces inflammation and stimulates the growth of healthy tissue. Research shows that slathering comfrey ointment on the afflicted ankle reduces pain, tenderness, and swelling just as well as the usual treatment, a prescription anti-inflammatory lotion called diclofenac gel.

After a week, comfrey users were better healed and had 92% less pain; the diclofenac group had an 84% drop. Steer clear of supplements that contain the herb, however—they could contribute to liver damage, warns the FDA.

Subdue Foot Aches

Think twice before you purchase pricey custom-made orthotics for heel pain known as plantar fasciitis, say foot experts.

Activities such as running, stair-climbing, and even walking can cause the plantar fascia, the flat band of tissue on the bottom of your foot, to swell, bruise, or tear. Most people heal within 6 months on their own. The good news is that those with acute cases of foot pain may do just fine with store-bought heel cups that cost only a few bucks.

Choose a firm version from your local drugstore, suggests Marlene Reid, DPM, spokesperson for the American Podiatric Medical Association. Also try regularly stretching the muscles in your foot to build strength and rolling your arch over a tennis ball or soup can to help ease the ache.

Stifle Surgery Pain

Got a root canal scheduled? Recuperating in a sunny, music-filled room will help take away some of the hurt. A review of 14 studies involving 489 patients found that those who listened to pleasant music felt less pain—and required fewer pain meds—than those who healed in silence.

"Music has about the same effect as one acetaminophen tablet," says study author M. Soledad Cepeda, MD, PhD, a Colombian researcher who worked with Tufts University Medical Center scientists. Rolling up the blinds also helps, report University of Pittsburgh doctors, who found that back surgery patients recovering in sunny rooms required 22% less pain medication and felt less stress than those in dimly lit ones.

Stop Nagging Neck Pain

The most common cause of a sore neck? Strained spinal muscles overtaxed by heavy lifting, sleeping in an uncomfortable position, or hunching over a desk. A nonsteroidal anti-inflammatory drug (NSAID) such as ibuprofen or aspirin can reduce painful inflammation, but new research shows that omega-3 fatty acids, the "healthy" fat found in fish, work just as well.

In a University of Pittsburgh study of people taking NSAIDs for long-term back and neck pain, researchers added a daily 2,400 mg dose of omega-3s to the patients' diets for 2 weeks. The researchers then asked study participants to taper off their NSAID use and continue with a daily dose of 1,200 mg of omega-3s for another 2 weeks. After a month, nearly two-thirds reported a significant improvement in pain.

Omega-3 fatty acids impede the production of chemical messengers called prostaglandins; these trigger pain and swelling, researchers say. Take 1,000 to 1,200 mg a day for a month or two to get relief. (Fish oils also break up blood platelets, so avoid this treatment if you're on blood thinners.)

3 Ways to Beat Back Pain

1. Wear a heating pad. A Johns Hopkins University study found that putting on a portable heat wrap 8 hours a day for 3 days reduced the intensity of back pain by 60%, compared with going without one (both groups were also taking pain medication). The benefit lasted for up to 2 weeks. . . .

2. You can also try a 600 to 1,200 mg dose of devil's claw. This African herb has a long history of medicinal use. In recent research, it has been shown—in a total of 10 studies involving 1,567 participants—to ease chronic lower-back pain. Take it 3 times a day (you can find it in vitamin stores). Devil's claw can cause an upset stomach in some people.

3. Exercise may sound like a bad idea, but a UCLA study of 610 men and women with chronic lower-back pain discovered that those who were active were 30% less likely to experience an increase in pain and disability than those who were inactive. People who fared the best did moderate types of exercise—swimming and walking, for example.

Sore Muscles? Attack the Problem from All Angles

Prep your body.

Take a mixture of isoleucine, leucine, and valine (amino acid supplements). In a study from Japan, 30 people who were given this combo before doing squats had far less muscle soreness and fatigue in the following days than exercisers who got a sugar pill. Branched-chain amino acids such as these work together to reduce muscle protein breakdown during exercise as well as stimulate muscle protein growth. . . .

Then try arnica pills.

In a study of 82 marathon runners, those who took five D30 arnica tablets twice a day (the day before, day of, and 3 days after their race) reported less soreness than those given a placebo treatment. The D30 supplement can be found in vitamin stores and may be labeled with its full plant name, *Arnica montana.*

Or, consider taking CoQ10.

If you're on cholesterol-lowering statins, they can block the production of the nutrient coenzyme Q10 (CoQ10). This enzyme is key to muscle cell function. You can replenish your stores by taking 100 mg daily. That dosage can slash soreness in half, according to a study of 38 people done at Stony Brook University Health Sciences Center.

| "Homeopathy is a remarkable medicine,
 however unbelievable it seems."

Homeopathy Is
Effective Medicine

Robert Ullman and Judyth Reichenberg-Ullman

Although the reasons for its success remain unknown, homeopathy is an effective medical practice, assert Robert Ullman and Judyth Reichenberg-Ullman in the following viewpoint. Despite its efficacy in controlled studies and clinical practice, homeopathic medicine nevertheless continues to be subject to debate and skepticism, the authors claim. Because homeopathy employs highly diluted poisons as medicine, successful treatments do seem miraculous, the authors maintain. Nonetheless, the authors reason, years of clinical practice have proven homeopathy's value. Ullman and Reichenberg-Ullman, licensed naturopathic physicians, board certified in homeopathy, are authors of The Patient's Guide to Homeopathic Medicine.

As you read, consider the following questions:

1. Why do Ullman and Reichenberg-Ullman find it implausible that homeopathy should remain an enigma to the medical world?

Robert Ullman and Judyth Reichenberg-Ullman, "Healing with Homeopathy: Incredible Medicine," *Townsend Letter*, May 2006. www.townsendletter.com. Reproduced by permission of the authors.

2. According to the authors, why have chemists decided that homeopathy cannot work?

3. In the authors' opinion, what is a sign that patients have received their simillimum?

Homeopathy is both effective and incredible at the same time, and it seems that no amount of double-blind, controlled studies or clinical cases seems able to set the issue to rest. Ever since [Samuel] Hahnemann first set out his theories in the *Organon of Medicine* in 1810, homeopathy has been the subject of controversy and debate. After nearly two hundred years of successful practice, that homeopathy should still be having problems with acceptance and that it should remain an enigma to the medical world seems implausible to us. Nevertheless, that is the current state of affairs.

The Homeopathy Debate

Discussing homeopathy for many people is akin to discussing religion and politics at the same time: many opinions, much speculation, and few conclusions. We are no exception, but we have had the benefit of practicing homeopathy for many years and seeing both our successes and our failures with patients. This experience allows us to come down on one side of the issue with a strong opinion about whether or not homeopathy is effective. Some who have never experienced homeopathy, either as practitioners or as patients, flatly deny that homeopathy could possibly work, while those who have experienced homeopathy declare it either miraculous or totally worthless or somewhere in between.

Clearly, our bias is that homeopathic medicine is effective when properly prescribed, and a partial or utter failure when misunderstood and misapplied. We have done our best to master homeopathic practice over the years, and we still have much to learn. We have seen enough success in practice, however, to know that homeopathy is a remarkable medicine, however unbelievable it seems.

What makes homeopathy seem incredible? A number of reasons exist that, individually, might not seem so unbelievable, but they add up, as we shall see. Some of homeopathy's remarkable virtues are also the very things that strain its credibility. What is true of homeopathy is truly incredible, in both senses of the word.

Poisons as Medicine

One of the biggest problems in understanding homeopathic medicine lies in homeopathy's choice of medicinal substances. Every natural substance is a possible homeopathic medicine, as long as it can produce symptoms in a healthy person. This is called the "law of similars" or "like cures like," the foundational principle of Samuel Hahnemann's theory of homeopathy. The symptoms a substance in nature can produce in a healthy person can be cured by that same substance in a sick person. If a substance doesn't produce any symptoms when given over and over to healthy volunteers, it doesn't make the grade. Only those substances capable of making one sick can also be candidates as medicines. Counterintuitive? You bet. Nevertheless, it's true.

Some of the best medicines in homeopathic practice come from the most poisonous substances in nature. Viewing a homeopathic pharmacy is like going on a global hunt for the most deadly agents in the natural world: toxic minerals like mercury (Mercurius), arsenic (Arsenicum), and lead (Plumbum); poisonous plants containing strychnine, such Nux vomica and Ignatia; hallucinogenic alkaloids from Belladonna and Datura (Stramonium); and animal poisons from a wide variety of insects (Apis, Cantharis), spiders (Tarentula, Theridion), snakes (Lachesis, Naja), sea animals (Murex, Medusa, Sepia), and scorpions (Androctonus). Two thousand or so additional mineral, plant, and animal substances of less virulence are also used in the making of homeopathic medicines. The idea of using poisons as medicine may give pause

Conditions Treated Most Often by Homeopaths and Conventional Doctors

Type of Physician

Homeopathic		Conventional	
Condition	% of Patients	Condition	% of Patients
Asthma	4.9	Hypertension	6.4
Depression	3.5	Upper respiratory	3.9
Otitis media	3.5	infection	
Allergic rhinitis	3.4	Otitis media	3.4
Headache and	3.2	Diabetes	2.9
migraine		Acute pharyngitis	2.6
Neurotic disorders	2.9	Chronic sinusitis	2.6
Allergy, non-specific	2.8	Bronchitis	2.6
Dermatitis	2.6	Sprains and strains	1.7
Arthritis	2.5	Back disorders	1.4
Hypertension	2.4	Allergic rhinitis	1.4

TAKEN FROM: Wayne B. Jones, et al., "A Critical Overview of Homeopathy," *Annals of Internal Medicine*, March 4, 2003.

to potential practitioners and patients alike. Nonetheless, these are some of the substances from which effective and non-toxic homeopathic medicines are made.

Astronomical Dilutions

As if the idea of using poisons is not enough to challenge credulity, the process that makes those poisons more acceptable makes homeopathy even more unbelievable. Such medicines are made non-toxic by diluting them. That seems reasonable: you make a poison less toxic by diluting it. The amount of dilution, however, is so astronomical that it seems that nothing could possibly remain of the original substance, thereby seeming to eliminate any possibility that the medicine could remain effective.

An extract of a substance used to make a C potency [base strength] of a homeopathic medicine, say table salt (Natrum muriaticum), is serially diluted one part to 99 parts, six, 12,

30, 200, 1,000, 10,000, or 50,000 times to make various potencies of the medicine. Theoretically, no molecules of the original substance remain past the twelfth dilution, because the dilution factor exceeds Avogadro's number (i.e., the number of molecules in a mole of the original substance). This is where the chemists decide that homeopathy can't work because "there's nothing left in that stuff!" Nevertheless, homeopathic medicines have been shown to be clinically effective in high dilutions. How is that possible? No one knows. Various theories have been proposed involving the memory of water and liquid crystals, but nothing has been definitively proved.

Because of proven clinical effectiveness of homeopathy in many, though not all, double-blind, placebo-controlled trials, some information must survive the dilution process to inform the body in such a way as to produce a therapeutic response. An unknown mechanism does not eliminate the possibility that the body is able to recognize the unique patterns of substances prepared homeopathically and to use them beneficially.

A Whole Lot of Shaking

One interesting fact to add to the dilution controversy is succussion, the process of shaking the vial between each dilution during the preparation process. Without succussion, the diluted medicines are not effective in producing clinical changes, especially in the higher dilutions. This implies that succussion alters the dilutions physically or chemically in some way that preserves the pattern of the original substance, allowing it to remain active clinically even when diluted far beyond the 12C potency.

In fact, higher dilutions, such as 200C, 1M, 10M, and 50M—which are prepared with a far greater number of dilutions and succussions—are considered by homeopaths to be more powerful and to last longer in clinical practice than the lower dilutions of 6C, 12C, and 30C.

One Medicine is All a Patient Needs

Another startling proposition of homeopathic medicine, especially when compared to conventional medicine, is that the one medicine that truly matches the chronic or constitutional symptoms of the patient will stimulate a substantial portion, if not all, of the healing that a patient needs—physically, mentally, and emotionally. Such a homeopathic medicine is called the simillimum, defined as the medicine most similar to the patient's symptoms. Having seen such results in many of our cases, we know this principle to be true, and it is what we strive to achieve with every patient. . . . We are not always able to find the simillimum for every patient and may have to settle for a series of homeopathic medicines that are approximations. These approximate medicines each cover a part of the symptom picture and thus do part of the job, but not the complete healing we know is possible with the single correct medicine. Other homeopathic medicines may be beneficial for acute illnesses or first aid, but nothing matches the comprehensive benefits of the simillimum.

The Laws of Cure

One sign that a patient may have received his or her simillimum is the return of symptoms experienced previously, perhaps years or decades earlier. These often come in the reverse order of their original appearance. The symptoms stay for a much shorter time than they had originally, although the time is proportionate to their original appearance. If observed carefully, this process may result in the reappearance of symptoms dating all the way back to infancy or even birth itself. The return of old symptoms is an excellent sign in homeopathic treatment, indicating that the medicine is producing results. Such a phenomenon is rarely seen in conventional medicine where either it would not be believed or would be misinterpreted as renewed illness rather than as part of a curative process.

Other observed indications of a healing process underway are skin eruptions and discharges occurring for no apparent reason. These seem to be part of the body's attempt to cleanse and heal itself in response to the stimulus of the homeopathic medicine. During the healing process, symptoms may also disappear from center to periphery, from top to bottom, and from most important to least important organs and functions. These directions of healing are known classically as the Laws of Cure. Although the healing processes may not occur in those exact ways in every case, they often fit at least part of that pattern described by the observant nineteenth century homeopath from Pennsylvania, Constantine Hering.

Another surprising and illogical, though common, event in homeopathic practice occurs when one dose of a homeopathic medicine produces effects for weeks, months, or even years. It appears that the medicine acts as a catalyst to a healing process that has a certain momentum specific to the particular combination of the person, the illness, and the medicine itself. During the indefinite period of that medicine's single dose action, symptoms are mitigated or they simply disappear. After that period, the symptoms may return until another dose of medicine is administered; in some cases, the symptoms may never return, leaving the patient in good health. A dose of a well selected homeopathic medicine that works perfectly will cure the patient of all the symptoms that it matches. Unbelievable, perhaps, but again, demonstrable in clinical practice.

Symptoms Borrowed from Nature

One interesting idea regarding homeopathy, recently proposed by Dr. Rajan Sankaran, is that the symptom picture of the homeopathic medicine is in a sense borrowed from the substance in nature from which the medicine is derived. The patient literally and metaphorically takes on the state of the substance in nature, producing the same physical and mental state that would be produced by actually being toxically affected by the substance, but without experiencing any actual contact with it. In this way, a person acquires symptoms from a substance, like an exotic mineral, plant, or animal, that may exist half-a-world away, without any conscious knowledge of the resulting state. During the homeopathic interview, when the patient is led into a process that reaches beyond the conscious mind, the nature of substance itself begins to be revealed by the patient's words and gestures. These words and gestures have nothing to do with the actual situation or conscious thoughts and feelings of the patient. Sankaran calls these symptoms non-human specific feelings and sensations that come directly from the substance itself. The patient may say, "I have no idea why I'm saying this," when referring to these sensations and thoughts, but those reactions often relate directly to the substance that the patient needs as medicine. For example, a patient needing a medicine from a bird may start to speak about being up above all her worries, flying freely. A patient who needs a mineral medicine may speak about his structure crumbling, thereby pointing to a substance like that within Arsenicum, a remedy used when a patient talks about fears of imminent death. A person may relate a sensation found characteristically only in patients needing a medicine from a certain plant family, such as the feeling of constriction and expansion found in medicines made from the cactus family.

Incredible but True

All the above discussion may cause a person to decide that homeopathy is just a hoax, a delusion, or simply an elaborate form of placebo. If so, use other forms of healing and be well.

For those of you who can willingly suspend your disbelief, we urge you to give homeopathy the benefit of the doubt and try it. . . .

If those remedies work, consult an experienced classical homeopath for your constitutional remedy, and, if you are given an effective medicine, watch your chronic illnesses and mental and emotional states improve and resolve over several months to a year. See for yourself if this incredible medicine produces the plausible results that we know are possible.

| "[The homeopathy] debate could go on for another 200 years, but to me it is entirely obvious. The remedies do not work."

Homeopathy Is Not Effective Medicine

Edzard Ernst

In the following viewpoint, Professor Edzard Ernst claims that homeopathic remedies are ineffective. Controlled studies show no difference in recovery rates between those who receive homeopathic medicines and those who receive a placebo, he maintains. Any improvement in the health of patients receiving homeopathic treatment is due to other factors, Ernst reasons. For example, homeopathic doctors often spend more time with their patients and are more empathetic. While homeopathic medicines do not cure patients, much could be learned from the way homeopathic practitioners interact with their patients, he concludes. Ernst, homeopathically trained, is chair of complementary medicine at the University of Exeter.

As you read, consider the following questions:

1. Why does Ernst feel so strongly about studying homeopathy?

Edzard Ernst, "Homeopathy Is Pointless, Says Expert," *Daily Mail* (UK), May 23, 2006. www.dailymail.co.uk. Reproduced by permission.

2. What does the author believe plays a great role in any drug's efficacy?

3. In the author's opinion, what is necessary in order to advance science and health care?

From Prince Charles to the new patient who has just had their first appointment with their local homeopath, there has never been a shortage of people raving about homeopathy's benefits and healing powers.

With labelling regulations set to change next year [in the United Kingdom in 2007]—bottles will be allowed to feature the remedies' uses and indications instead of just the confusing Latin name they carry at present—it is likely that the popularity of homeopathy will soar.

A Paradox

But in this field we have a paradox between the power of the human mind and the proof of science.

It cannot be disputed that, in a clinical sense, homeopathy seems to help patients. Yet, scientifically speaking, the remedies have absolutely no potency. I wasn't joking when I stated ... that you'd be better off with a glass of water than a homeopathic pill.

My remit is to research all forms of complementary medicine, but I personally feel very strongly about homeopathy because it is so popular, with about 3,000 registered homeopaths in the UK. Around 40 per cent of British doctors refer their patients to a homeopath.

Having worked in Germany's only homeopathic hospital in my youth, where I advocated the therapy's use, I have a good understanding of its principles. Certainly, I do not have any axe to grind against it.

During the 12 years of my research into the subject, countless contradictory studies have emerged, their conclusions swinging from one end of the scale to the other.

The Risks of Homeopathy

Homeopathy is to medicine what astrology is to astronomy: it's witchcraft ... While homeopathic medicine is not toxic, its use as an alternative to conventional medicine can, in fact, cause serious harm. ...

The risks of patients relying solely on homeopathy are obvious. Chronic constipation is [an] example. This can be evidence of bowel cancer and yet people can blithely go on treating it with homeopathy without realising the risks of not seeking medical attention. ...

Even more distressing is the story of one of my patients—a very personable young woman with breast cancer who keeps coming back to see me even though she doesn't accept any of my advice.

She could easily have been cured, but has refused surgery and conventional drugs in favour of hocus-pocus homeopathic remedies.

Her tumour is getting bigger and bigger and has pushed through her skin—there is now an ulcer where once there was a small lump. She dresses it with honey and God knows what else and she thinks it is getting better.

Michael Baum, "Homeopathy Is Worse Than Witchcraft—
And the NHS Must Stop Paying for It," Daily Mail (UK),
January 5, 2007. www.dailymail.co.uk.

For every study that says homeopathy works, there are a barrage of critics who state the opposite. For every study that claims it doesn't work, a whole host of people who have been 'cured' by the remedies retort back.

It is no wonder homeopathy has become a confusing and controversial matter, capable of fuelling endless debate.

Unravelling the Truth

But I now believe that, through rigorous trials of my own, combined with analysis of previous trials and an understanding of human psychology, I have unravelled the truth of this controversial medicine and of our own relationship with it.

Homeopathy is based on the theory of treating 'like with like', supposedly giving patients substances that cause the very same problems they are suffering from. Asthma, migraines, irritable bowel syndrome and hormonal imbalances are thought to benefit from the treatment.

The remedies are made using a complex process of diluting and shaking, which is disputable in itself. The process leaves the remedies so diluted there are often no molecules of the supposedly active substance in them.

The remedies have been mathematically likened to putting a glass of an active substance into the Atlantic at New York and then sampling the water in Southampton [UK].

And were it possible for any treatment to work without any active ingredient, then we would have to tear up all our physics books and start again.

One of the remedies I looked at in great detail was arnica, which is widely used by homeopaths to treat trauma of all sorts and to aid post-operatic healing.

Studying Homeopathic Remedies

During our study, we gave two different dilutions of arnica to two groups of patients, and gave a third group a placebo. All subjects had had the same operation.

We then measured and monitored their bruising, swelling and pain. There was absolutely no difference between the three groups and all three groups recovered at the same rate.

In another trial, I looked at the effect of homeopathic remedies on children suffering with asthma.

If any of our trials should have given the remedies a little helping hand it would have been this one, as not only is homeopathy a popular treatment for asthma, but children are also thought to respond better to it than adults.

Nonetheless, once more no differences were seen between the children who took the homeopathic remedies and the control group.

Even more importantly, we carried out a huge analysis of all other trials conducted to date. We summarised all studies on arnica.

In their totality, they failed to show that arnica is any more potent than a placebo. We drew the same conclusion with many other remedies.

Why Are People Convinced by Homeopathy?

The striking issue for scientists to consider is that patients do get better—which I know as a homeopath myself and from the people I've talked to. This requires an explanation.

I believe there are a number of factors that make homeopathy appear to work, but the potency of the remedies is not one of them.

The setting of the treatment is an important factor. Think about it this way. When you see a GP [general practitioner], you get ten minutes, if you're lucky, with someone who is busy and often harassed.

A typical first encounter with a homeopath is an hour-and-a-half and the practitioner is usually empathic and understanding. It's entirely conceivable that this encounter is, in itself, of therapeutic value. Certainly, patients tend to leave feeling reassured and optimistic.

The Placebo Effect

Which brings me on to the placebo effect. Expectation plays a great role in a drug's efficacy. It is only natural to believe a remedy is working when you've been prescribed it in a clinical setting from a professional.

And there's the fact you've handed over money for it, too.

We must then throw in what scientists call the 'natural history' of an illness. Most of the time, people get better anyway, but it seems easier to put your recovery down to your homeopath than your body's own healing powers.

This is certainly what has happened with many of the studies that have proven homeopathy to work.

Far too often, studies are conducted without control groups.

Were a control group included too, it would be obvious that recovery happens naturally.

Finally, add what is termed 'social desirability' into the mix. It takes a brave person to turn round and tell a homeopath that their remedies had no effect whatsoever. Most of us, fitted with an urge to be polite and a fear of being unkind, tend to give positive feedback.

So it seems that it is not the remedy, but the kindness, empathy and time of the practitioner and the patient's own will that bring about the healing effects.

From the patient's point of view, does it really matter what is happening as long as they get better? Probably not. But in order to advance science and health care, it is necessary to understand what is going on.

What We Can Learn

It is likely that this debate could go on for another 200 years, but to me it is entirely obvious. The remedies do not work.

What the studies show is that homeopaths are very good clinicians, working in a setting and manner that inspires confidence and expectation. As a result, they are maximising the placebo effect of the powerless remedies they prescribe.

So before we throw away our homeopathic remedies, we should look to the practitioners and see what we can learn from the way in which they work.

Other medics may benefit from learning from homeopaths, who manage to cure without an effective treatment.

Wouldn't it be wonderful if we could maximise this placebo effect with a treatment that actually works, such as a good old aspirin?

| *"Marijuana is effective at relieving nausea and vomiting, spasticity, appetite loss, certain types of pain, and other debilitating symptoms."*

Medical Marijuana Is an Effective Medicine

Lester Grinspoon

According to Lester Grinspoon in the following viewpoint, researchers have proven what medical practitioners have known since ancient times—marijuana is effective medicine. HIV patients suffering from the pain that accompanies nerve damage obtain relief from smoked marijuana, he claims. Studies also show that marijuana relieves nausea, appetite loss, and other painful symptoms that accompany debilitating diseases. Since pharmaceutical alternatives are often too expensive and lack the dosage control that smoked marijuana offers, the federal government should remove its irrational ban on medical marijuana. Grinspoon, professor of psychiatry at Harvard Medical School, is coauthor of Marihuana: The Forbidden Medicine.

As you read, consider the following questions:

1. To what conventional pain drugs is neuropathic pain resistant, in Grinspoon's view?

Lester Grinspoon, "Marijuana as Wonder Drug," *Boston.com*, March 1, 2007. www.boston.com. Reproduced by permission.

2. During what century does the author claim marijuana became a well-established Western medicine?

3. In the author's opinion, what are the advantages of smoking as a delivery system for medicinal marijuana?

A new study in the journal *Neurology* is being hailed as unassailable proof that marijuana is a valuable medicine. It is a sad commentary on the state of modern medicine—and US drug policy—that we still need "proof" of something that medicine has known for 5,000 years.

A Remedy for Neuropathic Pain

The study, from the University of California at San Francisco [UCSF], found smoked marijuana to be effective at relieving the extreme pain of a debilitating condition known as peripheral neuropathy. It was a study of HIV patients, but a similar type of pain caused by damage to nerves afflicts people with many other illnesses including diabetes and multiple sclerosis. Neuropathic pain is notoriously resistant to treatment with conventional pain drugs. Even powerful and addictive narcotics like morphine and OxyContin often provide little relief. This study leaves no doubt that marijuana can safely ease this type of pain.

As all marijuana research in the United States must be, the new study was conducted with government-supplied marijuana of notoriously poor quality. So it probably underestimated the potential benefit.

This is all good news, but it should not be news at all. In the 40-odd years I have been studying the medicinal uses of marijuana, I have learned that the recorded history of this medicine goes back to ancient times and that in the 19th century it became a well-established Western medicine whose versatility and safety were unquestioned. From 1840 to 1900, American and European medical journals published over 100 papers on the therapeutic uses of marijuana, also known as cannabis.

Of course, our knowledge has advanced greatly over the years. Scientists have identified over 60 unique constituents in marijuana, called cannabinoids, and we have learned much about how they work. We have also learned that our own bodies produce similar chemicals, called endocannabinoids.

A Mountain of Evidence

The mountain of accumulated anecdotal evidence that pointed the way to the present and other clinical studies also strongly suggests there are a number of other devastating disorders and symptoms for which marijuana has been used for centuries; they deserve the same kind of careful, methodologically sound research. While few such studies have so far been completed, all have lent weight to what medicine already knew but had largely forgotten or ignored: Marijuana is effective at relieving nausea and vomiting, spasticity, appetite loss, certain types of pain, and other debilitating symptoms. And it is extraordinarily safe—safer than most medicines prescribed every day. If marijuana were a new discovery rather than a well-known substance carrying cultural and political baggage, it would be hailed as a wonder drug.

The pharmaceutical industry is scrambling to isolate cannabinoids and synthesize analogs, and to package them in non-smokable forms. In time, companies will almost certainly come up with products and delivery systems that are more useful and less expensive than herbal marijuana. However, the analogs they have produced so far are more expensive than herbal marijuana, and none has shown any improvement over the plant nature gave us to take orally or to smoke.

The Advantages of Smoked Marijuana

We live in an antismoking environment. But as a method of delivering certain medicinal compounds, smoking marijuana has some real advantages: The effect is almost instantaneous, allowing the patient, who after all is the best judge, to fine-tune his or her dose to get the needed relief without intoxication. Smoked marijuana has never been demonstrated to have serious pulmonary consequences, but in any case the technology to inhale these cannabinoids without smoking marijuana already exists as vaporizers that allow for smoke-free inhalation.

Hopefully the UCSF study will add to the pressure on the US government to rethink its irrational ban on the medicinal use of marijuana—and its destructive attacks on patients and caregivers in states that have chosen to allow such use. Rather than admit they have been mistaken all these years, federal officials can cite "important new data" and start revamping outdated and destructive policies. The new Congress could go far in establishing its bona fides as both reasonable and compassionate by immediately moving on this issue.

Such legislation would bring much-needed relief to millions of Americans suffering from cancer, AIDS, multiple sclerosis, arthritis, and other debilitating illnesses.

> *"There is no scientific evidence that qualifies smoked marijuana to be called medicine."*

Medical Marijuana Is Not an Effective Medicine

Andrea Barthwell

In the following viewpoint, Andrea Barthwell, former deputy director at the White House Office of National Drug Control Policy, maintains that there is no scientific evidence that smoked marijuana is good medicine. Marijuana may make patients feel better, but marijuana has no scientifically proven capacity to serve as a medicine, she argues. Moreover, Barthwell asserts, smoking itself is harmful and thus a poor method for administering the active chemical in marijuana. Barthwell, a medical doctor, is a consultant for GW Pharmaceuticals, which manufactures Sativex, a marijuana extract spray.

As you read, consider the following questions:

1. According to Barthwell, between what must modern medicine distinguish when it comes to medicine?
2. What are the limitations of synthetic versions of the active ingredient in marijuana, in the author's opinion?

Andrea Barthwell, "A Haze of Misinformation Clouds Issue of Medical Marijuana," *Los Angeles Times*, July 22, 2003, p. B13. Reproduced by permission of the author.

3. Under what conditions are even dangerous substances allowed to be used medicinally, in the author's view?

As a physician with more than 20 years of experience dealing with patients who are addicted to drugs, I am often asked my professional opinion about a contentious public health question: What is the medical basis for smoking marijuana? The answer needs some context.

Research, Testing, and Oversight

Americans today have the world's safest, most effective system of medical practice, built on a process of scientific research, testing and oversight that is unequaled.

Before the passage of the Pure Food and Drug Act in 1907, Americans were exposed to a host of patent medicine "cure-alls," everything from vegetable "folk remedies" to dangerous mixtures with morphine. The major component of most "cures" was alcohol, which probably explained why people reported that they "felt better."

Needless to say, claimed benefits were erratic and irreproducible.

Marijuana, whatever its value, is intoxicating, and it's not surprising that sincere people will report relief of their symptoms when they smoke it. The important point is that there is a difference between feeling better and actually getting better. It is the job of modern medicine to establish this distinction.

The debate over drug use generates a great deal of media attention—including the focus on the administration's appeal to the U.S. Supreme Court against medical marijuana—and frequent misinformation. Some will have read, for instance, that the medicinal value of smoking marijuana represents "mainstream medical opinion." It is time to set the record straight.

The Truth About Medical Marijuana

- Marijuana is a dangerous, addictive drug that poses significant health threats to users.

- Marijuana has no medical value that can't be met more effectively by legal drugs.

- Marijuana users are far more likely to use other drugs like cocaine and heroin than non-marijuana users.

- Drug legalizers use "medical marijuana" as [a] red herring in [an] effort to advocate broader legalization of drug use.

"Exposing the Myth of Smoked Medical Marijuana,"
U.S. Drug Enforcement Administration, www.usdoj.gov/dea.

Setting the Record Straight

Simply put, there is no scientific evidence that qualifies smoked marijuana to be called medicine. Further, there is no support in the medical literature that marijuana, or indeed any medicine, should be smoked as the preferred form of administration. The harms to health are simply too great.

Marijuana advocates often cite the 1999 National Academy of Science's Institute of Medicine report as justifying the drug's medical use. But, in fact, the verdict of that report was "marijuana is not a modern medicine." The institute was particularly troubled by the notion that crude marijuana might be smoked by patients, which it termed "a harmful drug-delivery system."

These concerns are echoed by the Food and Drug Administration, the agency charged with approving all medicines. As the FDA recently noted: "While there are no proven benefits to [smoked] marijuana use, there are many short- and long-term risks associated with marijuana use."

Compounds in the marijuana plant do potentially have a medical value. For instance, a synthetic version of an ingredient in marijuana has been approved for treating nausea for chemotherapy patients, as well as for treatment of anorexia associated with weight loss in patients with AIDS.

Admittedly, these medications have limitations, including the relatively slow onset of relief. Researchers are exploring drug-delivery systems that allow rapid relief—perhaps an oral inhalator like those used by asthma patients—as a response to patient needs.

No Proven Medicinal Value

But these medications are a far cry from burning the crude weed and gulping down the smoke. Every American is familiar with aspirin, and some know that it was first found in willow bark, from which the therapeutic agent acetylsalicylic acid was eventually synthesized. Surely no one today would chew willow bark, much less smoke a piece of tree, to cure a headache.

Medical science does not fear any compound, even those with a potential for abuse. If a substance has the proven capacity to serve a medical purpose, then it will be accepted. We have done so with substances as dangerous as opium, allowing the medical use of many of its derivatives, including morphine, Demerol and OxyContin. The key term is "proven capacity." Only if compounds from marijuana pass the same tests of research scrutiny that any other drug must undergo will they become part of the modern medical arsenal.

Our investment in medical science is at risk if we do not defend the proven process by which medicines are brought to the market. All drugs must undergo rigorous clinical trials before a drug can be released for public use.

The overarching charge to any physician is: "First, do no harm." That is the test smoked marijuana cannot pass.

Periodical Bibliography

The following articles have been selected to supplement the diverse views presented in this chapter.

Kimball C. Atwood IV   "The Ongoing Problem with the National Center for Complementary and Alternative Medicine," *Skeptical Inquirer*, September/October 2003.

Marcus Conant   "Guest Editorial: Medical Marijuana," *Family Practice News*, July 1, 2005.

Len Costa   "Alternative Medicine," *Best Life*, December 2006.

Sarah Glazer   "Homeopathy Debate," *CQ Researcher*, December 19, 2003.

Harvard Health Letter   "Reefer Rx: Marijuana As Medicine," September 2004.

Issues & Controversies   "Herbal Supplements," December 13, 2004.

Issues & Controversies   "Medical Marijuana Update," July 8, 2005.

Wayne B. Jonas, Ted J. Kaptchuk, and Klaus Linde   "A Critical Overview of Homeopathy," *Annals of Internal Medicine*, March 4, 2003.

Arthur Jones   "Searchers Follow Ancient Traditions," *National Catholic Reporter*, May 6, 2005.

Patrick Marshall   "Marijuana Laws," *CQ Researcher*, February 11, 2005.

Alice Miles   "Opinion: Alternative Medicine Is Too Silly to Regulate," *The Times* (UK), March 3, 2004.

Robert M. Sade   "Complementary and Alternative Medicine: Foundations, Ethics, and Law," *Journal of Law, Medicine & Ethics*, Summer 2003.

William Triplett   "Dietary Supplements," *CQ Researcher*, September 3, 2004.

CHAPTER 3

Are New Medical Technologies and Policies Beneficial?

Chapter Preface

Most scientists agree that research using new genetic technologies should proceed cautiously, but some fear that laws criminalizing this research are dangerous and represent a step backward for science. According to Paul Berg, who won the Nobel Prize in chemistry in 1980 for his work on recombinant DNA, "Criminalizing pure science is an absurd throwback to prohibitions on speaking out on scientific issues or new truths."

Throughout history, people have frequently reacted to advances in technology with fear, which in turn has often been followed by attempts to ban and sometimes make it a crime to practice these advances. In 1734, the French philosopher Voltaire argued for experimental inoculation against smallpox. He asked French leaders to consider "the benefits to be gained by applying our knowledge of nature to the knowable and remediable causes of human suffering," claims historian Alan Charles Kors. In response, the French government consulted two well-respected authorities at the University of Paris: the Faculty of Medicine and the Faculty of Theology. According to Kors, the Faculty of Medicine believed that "[inoculation] would take us into uncharted and dangerous seas of innovation beyond the control of rightful authority. It would vitiate the sorts of traditions that had kept us decent and humane." The Faculty of Theology argued that inoculation was an attempt to play God. For them, Kors explains, "Inoculation was an act of hubris, a wanton and insolent human intrusion on God's domain, and if we crossed that line, how would we ever find our way back to our rightful place in the natural order?" As a result of these views, inoculating people against smallpox remained a crime in France until King Louis XV died of the disease on May 10, 1774.

Arguments similar to those advocated by the Faculties of Medicine and Theology in eighteenth-century France have been expressed concerning research that utilizes cloning. In fact, since the beginning of the millennium, each session of Congress has proposed a law that would make it a crime to use any form of human cloning, including therapeutic cloning for stem cell research. Genetic researchers hope that stem cell research will lead to cures for debilitating diseases such as Parkinson's, Alzheimer's, and diabetes. Nevertheless, despite its potential to, using Voltaire's words, "relieve human suffering," therapeutic cloning would become a crime under proposed laws. Under the most recent proposal, which as of June 2007 remains in committee, anyone who performed or participated in human cloning would be imprisoned for up to 10 years. Moreover, if cloning was conducted for "pecuniary gain," that is, for payment, participants could pay a fine of not less that $1 million.

Kors and others who oppose such laws fear that the government will make the same mistake as that made by the French Crown. According to Kors, if the government criminalizes biomedical research such as therapeutic cloning, "We have criminalized the effort both to understand nature and to make that knowledge available to those who choose to use it voluntarily and peacefully. We have criminalized the pursuit of knowledge that could alleviate human agony." Other commentators are more optimistic. Noretta Koertge, professor of the science history and philosophy at Indiana University, asserts, "Any attempt to undermine science will, in the long run, be unsuccessful in this country. Americans place too high a value on medical advances to stifle research in that area—or so I hope."

Whether laws criminalizing medical technologies such as therapeutic cloning will impede scientific progress is subject to debate. The authors in the following chapter debate the appropriateness of other medical technologies and policies.

| *"The HPV vaccine is extremely effect-ive ..."*

The Human Papillomavirus Vaccine Is a Beneficial Medical Breakthrough

Jonathan L. Temte

In the following viewpoint, Jonathan L. Temte asserts that the human papillomavirus (HPV) vaccine is an excellent medical tool. HPV, the most common sexually transmitted disease, infects over 50 percent of females and is responsible for 70 percent of women with cervical cancer. Vaccinating girls in early adolescence will not only help prevent HPV, Temte reasons, but also gives doctors an opportunity to educate them about safe sexual behaviors. Temte is a professor of medicine at the University of Wisconsin School of Medicine and Public Health.

As you read, consider the following questions:

1. At what age does the ACIP recommend girls be given the HPV vaccine?

2. In Temte's opinion, what are some of the consequences of HPV infection?

Jonathan L. Temte, "HPV Vaccine: A Cornerstone of Female Health," *American Family Physician*, vol. 75, p. 28. Copyright © 2007 American Academy of Family Physicians. Reproduced by permission.

3. What, in the author's view, reduces the benefit of using the HPV vaccine as a starting point for educational interventions?

A medical intervention that is a true preventive tool and a good reason for anticipatory guidance and education does not come along often; the new human papillomavirus (HPV) vaccine is both. In June 2006, the Centers for Disease Control and Prevention's Advisory Committee on Immunization Practices (ACIP) recommended universal administration of three doses of the quadrivalent HPV vaccine (Gardasil) in girls 11 or 12 years of age. The recommendation also allows physicians, at their discretion, to immunize girls as young as nine years and to vaccinate women up to 26 years of age.

Significant Consequences

HPV is ubiquitous in human populations. Of the more than 40 serotypes of HPV known to cause genital infections, four (types 6, 11, 16, and 18) are responsible for approximately 70 percent of cervical cancer cases and 90 percent of genital wart cases in the United States. HPV acquisition occurs rapidly after the initiation of sexual activity. Fifty-four percent of females have been shown to have HPV infection within four years of first sexual intercourse. Moreover, sexual activity commences early in the United States: 29.3 percent of ninth-grade girls report prior sexual activity, a number that increases to 62.4 percent by 12th grade. Consequently, HPV infection is the most common sexually transmitted disease (STD) in American youth.

HPV infection has significant consequences. In 2002, there were approximately 14,000 new cases of cervical cancer and 4,000 deaths from the disease, making it the 11th most common cancer in U.S. women. In addition, an estimated 300,000 high-grade and 1 million low-grade squamous intraepithelial lesions are detected each year, leading to multiple follow-up visits and invasive procedures (e.g., colposcopies, cervical biopsies). HPV infection accounts for expenditures of more than $2 billion per year and significantly affects patient privacy and comfort.

The HPV vaccine is extremely effective, especially when it is provided before acquisition of the targeted serotypes. The vaccine prevents over 95 percent of HPV infections caused by serotypes 6, 11, 16, and 18, thus blocking the initial pathogenic step that leads to 70 percent of cervical cancers. Therefore, immunization before the initiation of sexual activity is of paramount importance. Later immunization can still provide protection, depending on the patient's history of HPV exposure. Although the vaccine can significantly reduce the incidence of cervical pathology, screening with Papanicolaou smears should continue because of the potential effects of HPV serotypes not covered by the vaccine.

Anticipatory Guidance

The ACIP recommendation capitalizes on the extremely low likelihood of prior sexual activity in early-adolescent girls and facilitates the delivery of two other recommended vaccines (i.e., tetravalent meningococcal conjugate vaccine [MCV4; Menactra] and tetanus toxoid, reduced diphtheria toxoid, and acellular pertussis booster [Tdap; Boostrix, Adacel]). Together, these three vaccines provide the opportunity for important anticipatory guidance during early adolescence.

The onset of adolescence often is a time when patients generally are in relatively good health and do not visit their physicians; the majority of adolescent visits are for acute illness and injury. Nevertheless, patients need anticipatory behavioral guidance during adolescence. There is good evidence that educational interventions effectively reduce STD risk. Although there is no recommendation for a routine early adolescence visit, the American Academy of Family Physicians endorses discussing substance use (e.g., tobacco, alcohol), obesity,

Public Support for the HPV Vaccine

- 61% of parents or guardians of girls under the age of 18 said they would want their daughter to receive the HPV vaccine, whereas 6% would never want their daughter to receive the vaccine and 32% were not sure.

- 77% of all adults polled were in favor of providing information about the HPV vaccine in health education classes in schools, compared with 6% who opposed it and 16% who were not sure.

- 51% of all adults polled agreed that the HPV vaccine should be part of the vaccination routine for all children, whereas 21% disagreed and 28% were not sure.

The Wall Street Journal Online/
Harris Interactive Health-Care Poll, *July 2006.*

physical activity, and STDs with adolescent patients. The new HPV vaccination recommendation is an excellent starting point for enhancing these discussions. The potential benefit of this starting point is reduced, however, because the prevention and anticipatory guidance is targeted only at girls. Therefore, there is a need to further evaluate the effectiveness of this vaccine in males and to thoughtfully develop a routine early adolescence preventive health care visit for both sexes in family medicine settings.

"[Human papillomavirus] might be a good candidate for compulsory vaccination, but it's far too soon for states to order it now."

The Human Papillomavirus Vaccine Is Untested

Arthur Allen

Before states in the United States make the human papillomavirus (HPV) vaccine mandatory, Arthur Allen asserts in the following viewpoint, the manufacturer must provide further evidence of its safety and effectiveness. Parents are reluctant to vaccinate young daughters who are not yet sexually active when the vaccine has been tested on so few. Moreover, Allen maintains, to mandate that schoolgirls be vaccinated against HPV, states must be able to provide the expensive vaccine to those whose parents cannot afford it, and few states can afford to do so. Allen, a science writer, is author of Vaccine: The Controversial Story of Medicine's Greatest Lifesaver.

As you read, consider the following questions:

1. In Allen's opinion, why are religious conservatives opposed to the HPV vaccine?

2. Why is it easier for some people to believe that they will not need a vaccine, in the author's view?

3. What does the author claim is the main reason for any mandate?

Jon Abramson, chairman of the Centers for Disease Control and Prevention's (CDC) Advisory Committee for Immunization Practices, would seem like a logical proponent of compulsory vaccination against the human papillomavirus, or HPV. The virus causes cervical cancer, and Merck's Gardasil vaccine proved in trials to be safe and to prevent two-thirds of the growths leading to such cancers. Abramson's committee, whose pronouncements are followed religiously in the public health world, has already *recommended* that sixth-grade girls get three shots of HPV vaccine.

The Next Step?

So compulsory vaccination seems like the next step. HPV leads to cancers that kill 3,700 women each year and sicken another 6,000. That's a lot of death, misery, and medical expense—certainly more than what's caused by diseases like mumps or chicken pox, for which vaccination became mandatory in the 1980s and late '90s, respectively.

Merck launched a major direct-to-consumer advertising campaign after its vaccine was licensed [in the spring of 2006], and it lobbied fiercely to get state legislatures to mandate the vaccine. But HPV, unlike, say, chicken pox, spreads only through sex—so, naturally, vaccination has its opponents: Religious conservatives worry that it would make teens likelier to sin (by easing the threat of an STD [sexually transmitted disease]). Of course, vaccines don't put ants in your pants anymore than safety belts cause road rage, and, besides, nearly everyone gets laid eventually. The purpose of public health is to protect *everyone*, and the vaccination of young girls is based on solid data showing that 13 percent of girls have al-

The Bottom Line

The HPV vaccine is an important development in the nation's effort to prevent a form of cancer that infects and kills a small number of women every year. But its significant costs and the uncertainties of its long-term effectiveness more than outweigh making it mandatory at this stage.

A wiser course would be to focus resources on raising awareness about HPV in young women and encourage those who are sexually active to be routinely screened. Meanwhile, public health advocates and legislators should closely monitor Gardasil's effectiveness in teens and young adults who voluntarily agree to try it.

Mike King, "HPV Vaccine: Review Profit vs. Protection,"
Atlanta Journal Constitution, March 8, 2007. www.ajc.com.

ready had sex by the time they turn 15. (It's important to vaccinate before sexual debut, because HPV infection risk increases about 15 percent with each new partner.)

Yet Abramson—and most of the other leading vaccinologists—opposes *requiring* HPV vaccination for school entry. "I do not think that HPV should be mandated at this time," says Abramson, who is also a professor of pediatrics at Wake Forest University School of Medicine.

A Three-Way Dance

Abramson is right. HPV might be a good candidate for compulsory vaccination, but it's far too soon for states to order it now. To understand why, you have to grasp the slow, three-way dance that builds public support for vaccination programs.

Vaccines, unlike other medicines, are "imperfect" goods, in the economic sense. When you're sick, you want to buy a drug—whether it's an antibiotic for strep throat, chemotherapy for cancer, or insulin for your diabetes. But vaccines—with a few exceptions, such as Jonas Salk's 1955 polio vaccine, which was balm to the soul of a polio-panicked nation—aren't an obvious sell. When you bring your baby to the pediatrician, he or she is healthy. A vaccine, like any other medicine, has a (small) chance of causing a side effect, so there's a risk analysis to impose on a healthy infant. What's more, as vaccines eliminate the diseases they are designed to fight, it's easier to believe you won't need them. As a parent, especially one who reads scary websites that blame vaccines for things they aren't to blame for, a vaccine might not seem like an unalloyed benefit.

For the commonweal, however, the benefit is clear. The diseases we vaccinate our children against—such as rubella, measles, and whooping cough—can and will come back if we stop vaccinating against them. So it falls to states—federal and professional medical organizations offer advice on vaccines, but states lay down the law—to choose which vaccines are mandatory. But before public health officials mandate a vaccine, they must be able to buy it for those who can't afford it. At $360 for the series, Gardasil is very expensive. And President Bush's new budget cuts federal vaccine-purchasing aid; states can barely afford to pay for currently mandated vaccines against diseases like hepatitis B and pneumonia, let alone spring for Gardasil. "I certainly would not want to see a child removed from school because their parents could not afford the vaccine," says Abramson (who stresses that his CDC committee has not taken an official position on the mandate).

Then, too, though it is legitimate to ask parents to contribute to the public good, you can't push too hard for acceptance of a new vaccine—especially one like Gardasil, which has been tested on only about 20,000 women, including just 1,500 young girls. Parents may be willing to accept that their daughters will have sex at some point, but they may still (quite reasonably) believe that it won't be in the sixth grade. Why not wait a few years?

A Measure of Patience

Like all new medicines, HPV vaccine will contribute to cultural as well as medical change. That is why its introduction calls for a measure of patience. It's understandable that Merck—a very good vaccine maker—would like to corner a big share of the market before competitor GlaxoSmithKline's HPV vaccine is licensed later [in 2007]. Incentives to Big Pharma [the large pharmaceutical corporations] including mandatory vaccination, are part of what keep them in the business of making vaccines. But one would have hoped that Merck learned its lesson after pushing for broad use of Vioxx—a drug whose side effects wouldn't have been as problematic if they were occurring in only people who desperately needed the drug for pain medication.

In the case of HPV, demand from parents and young women will presumably boost sales enough to provide good data, over a few years, on whether Gardasil is as safe and effective as it seems. If it is, then popular support will slowly build for the mandate to get the vaccine to the girls who need it. And since mandates increase vaccine coverage by just 10 to 20 percent (in most states, people can opt out of vaccination if they are strongly opposed to it), it hardly seems prudent to reignite a culture war issue until there's a long trail of documentation to support vaccination.

To be sure, there is a moral argument for immediacy working against the practical one for patience: The main reason for any mandate is to get the vaccine to children whose parents aren't aware it exists until they are forced to get their child immunized. In the case of HPV, there is probably a large overlap between the daughters of such parents and the women whose lack of access to medical care leads to cancer (regular pap smears can detect cancerous growths caused by HPV, and such growths can be removed if caught early enough).

But, by applying overly vigorous and premature pressure, Merck hurt this cause in the short term by cheesing off public health officials, state legislators, and a variety of vaccine-skeptical parents around the country, before finally ending its lobbying campaign. Building consensus for compulsory vaccination in states across the country takes time and persuasion, and now, because of Merck's zeal, it will take even more.

> "[E]mbryonic stem cells offer the hope
> of new treatments for some very un-
> pleasant degenerative diseases."

Embryonic Stem Cell Research May Lead to Medical Advances

Ian Wilmut

According to Ian Wilmut in the following viewpoint, embryonic stem cells from cloned human embryos allow researchers to study the cellular development of intractable genetic diseases. For example, embryonic stem-cell research may explain how cells susceptible to motor neuron diseases mutate into the cells that cause neurodegeneration. In the future, Wilmut maintains, transplants of healthy cells derived from embryonic stem cells will treat patients with cardiovascular disease, type 1 diabetes, and other degenerative diseases. Wilmut, who led the team that cloned Dolly the sheep, conducts research at the Roslin Institute in Scotland.

As you read, consider the following questions:

1. When he and his colleague applied for a license to clone human embryos, what does Wilmut claim was *not* their goal?

2. What does the author claim is the prognoses for those who have motor neuron disease?

3. In the author's opinion, what will be necessary before successful embryonic stem-cell therapies can be developed?

The ability to derive embryonic stem cells from cloned human embryos and to control their differentiation into different cell types provides revolutionary new opportunities in biology and medicine. These methods make it possible to study human genetic diseases in entirely new ways and, in the longer term, such cells may be used in the treatment of human disease. Certainly this approach will provide opportunities that are not otherwise available.

Significant Steps

[In 2004] Professor Woo-Suk Hwang in Korea made a significant step forward when he derived stem cells from a cloned human embryo, demonstrating for the first time both that it was possible to clone human cells, and that it was possible to obtain embryonic stem cells from the resulting clone. . . .[1]

I, along with Christopher Shaw at the Institute of Psychiatry, King's College London, applied to the British government for a license to clone human embryos. That license was awarded on February 8, [2005]. Yet contrary to the public consternation that then arose, our goal is not to "clone babies," but rather to understated how nerve cell development goes awry in patients with motor neuron disease (MND), also called amyotrophic lateral sclerosis (ALS) or Lou Gehrig disease.

It is our hope that we will obtain new understanding of, and develop the first effective treatments for a very unpleasant

1. In December 2005 it was discovered that Hwang's cloned stem cell lines were fakes, and Hwang's research was discredited. This news has not altered Wilmut's views on the value of embryonic stem cell research.

disease for which there currently is no treatment. Whether this will happen by being able to test new drugs or by establishing a strategy for cell therapy we cannot predict. Either way, our experience with nuclear transfer will also have wider application. I anticipate that within 10 years, stem cell therapies will be available for some diseases and that in some cases the cells may be derived from cloned embryos. In the meantime, we need more funding for research, and a clarified, international regulatory landscape.

Treating MND

Motor neuron disease [MND] is a relentlessly progressive muscle-wasting disease that causes severe disability from the outset, and death usually within three to five years. Every year, 1,200 people in the United Kingdom die of MND and at present there is no drug treatment that significantly improves survival. Degeneration of motor neurons is the common cause of this fatal condition, but the etiology of the disease is not fully understood. It seems likely that several genetic and environmental factors contribute to the disease's pathogenesis.

The great majority of MND cases are sporadic, but between 5% and 10% are inherited. Among these familiar cases, mutations in the gene that encodes superoxide dismutase (SOD1) account for approximately 20% of cases, but genetic analyses suggest that at least four other genes remain to be identified.

Researchers initially assumed MND was caused by reduced SOD1 activity but this seems not to be the case. Mice in which the endogenous SOD1 gene has been deleted do not develop MND, whereas those that express mutant forms of the human gene develop paralysis. As the transgenic mice carrying the human gene also had their own two copies of the gene, this observation suggests that the effect of the mutation is through a cytotoxic effect of the abnormal protein, rather than a loss of function.

Moving from Mouse to Man

To progress in our studies, however, we'll have to move from mouse to man. There are several new potential sources of human cells liable to MND that may reveal the means by which abnormal *SOD*1 causes neurodegeneration. If preimplantation genetic screening is practiced for those cases in which the mutation has been identified, then embryonic stem cells could be derived from those embryos identified as carrying the mutation. This is not known to be happening at present, but is certainly technically feasible. Alternatively, known mutations could be introduced into embryonic stem cells derived from embryos not known to be liable to MND, and subsequently the MND cells contrasted with the original line.

My group at Roslin Institute and Dr. Shaw's group at the Institute of Psychiatry are using this latter approach in the first part of our collaborative project. This will provide us with the first opportunity to look for the effects of the abnormal protein on the structure and function of nerve cells equivalent to those of a young baby. At present there is no possibility of carrying out that research, so we have no idea what changes occur at this stage in a patient's life, when there are no clinical symptoms.

In those MND cases that are familial, yet in which the mutation has not been identified (8% of all cases), nuclear transfer will also offer new opportunities by enabling us to produce cloned embryos and cells that are genetically identical to those of the patient. Those cells will be vulnerable to the disease, even though we do not know the gene or genes responsible for causing it.

Once embryonic stem cell lines that are vulnerable to MND have been derived—whatever gene causes the disease— they will be differentiated into neural populations by groups working with Professor Shaw in London, and Jim McWhir of the Roslin Institute. These groups will then analyze the cells to determine the mechanisms that underlie motor neuron degeneration and develop a drug-screening program. Using high-throughput screening systems it will be possible to assess several hundred drugs comparatively cheaply.

The same approach could be used to study any human genetic disease, as long as the affected cell types can be produced from embryonic stem cells in the laboratory. The advantage is greatest if the mutation that causes the disease is not known. Candidate conditions for study include cardiomyopathy and some forms of cancer. It is also likely that genetic differences contribute to the "sporadic" cases of diseases such as ALS, in which direct inheritance is not apparent, perhaps by increasing vulnerability to environmental effects. If this is the case, then nuclear transfer may also be used to obtain cells from such families.

Cells for Therapy

In the longer term, embryonic stem cells offer the hope of new treatments for some very unpleasant degenerative diseases. These diseases include cardiovascular disease, spinal cord injury, Parkinson disease, and type 1 diabetes. Methods for the derivation of specific cells types from stem cells lines are being established in our laboratories at Roslin Institute, though it remains to be confirmed that they function normally after being transferred into a patient. In addition, a great deal remains to be learned about the most effective means of introducing the cells into patients.

In any treatment regimen it will be essential to avoid immunological rejection of the transplanted cells, but the immune response is likely to vary from one disease to another. Cells from cloned embryos would be most valuable in conditions such as cardiovascular disease, in which immune rejection could be avoided by transfer of histocompatible cells. By contrast, in the treatment of diseases within the central nervous system cells there is some uncertainty as to whether or not they would be subject to rejection. Finally, several of the conditions that are mentioned as candidates for cell therapy are autoimmune diseases, including diabetes type 1. In such cases, transfer of immunologically identical cells to a patient is expected to induce the same rejection.

An International Regulatory Framework

At present, cloning methods are repeatable and used by many laboratories around the world. Yet they are inefficient. This low overall efficiency reflects a failure of current procedures to reprogram the gene expression patterns from those appropriate for an adult cell to that required for normal embryonic development. We do not yet know whether similar abnormalities in gene expression would occur in stem cells derived from cloned embryos. Thus, the first use of cells from cloned embryos should be for research, and not to develop therapies.

Ultimately, such therapies will come, albeit not for many years—but not unless we can develop a clear, coherent, international regulatory framework. At present there are considerable differences between countries in the regulation of nuclear transfer to produce human embryos. In the United Kingdom, projects to derive cells from cloned embryos may be approved by the regulatory authority for the study of serious diseases. Human reproductive cloning, however, is illegal. A similar legal framework exists in some other countries, such as Sweden. In the United States, federal funds cannot be used for research with cloned embryos, but a referendum in California committed taxpayers in that state to massive expenditure over the next 10 years. Research with stem cells from donated embryos is very active in several Asian countries such as Singapore, Japan, and China. Recent action by the United Nations recommended that human cloning of any kind should be banned, but this is only advisory and the British government has made it clear it will not prohibit research of the kind that we are just beginning.

Regardless of what you believe about therapeutic applications, however, these cells will be an extremely important research resource. Cloned embryonic stem cells could allow researchers a glimpse into intractable genetic diseases that cannot be obtained in any other way, especially those for which no defined mutations have been discovered. Biomedicine should forge ahead to find out what it can learn from these unique research tools.

> "The promised miraculous [embryonic stem cell] cures have not materialized even for mice, much less men."

Claims of Embryonic Stem Cell Cures Are Exaggerated

Maureen L. Condic

Those who advocate research using embryonic stem cells from cloned human embryos have exaggerated their potential as cures, asserts Maureen L. Condic in the following viewpoint. Serious scientific problems remain before cures will materialize, if ever. Although scientists have been able to produce cells derived from embryonic stem cells, Condic claims, scientists have not proven that these cells will cure targeted diseases. Condic, professor of neurobiology and anatomy at the University of Utah School of Medicine, is conducting research on regeneration of the nervous system.

As you read, consider the following questions:

1. In Condic's view, why do human eggs not survive cloning procedures when animal eggs do sometimes survive?

2. According to the author, why do embryonic stem cell advocates dismiss the threat of tumors?

3. How is the hubris of scientists even more evident today, in the author's opinion?

Back at the beginning of 2002, there was considerable optimism regarding the promise that embryonic stem cells were said to hold for millions of people suffering from fatal or debilitating medical conditions. Stem cells derived from human embryos, it was claimed, provided the best hope for relief of human suffering. Despite the profound ethical concerns regarding the use of human embryos for medical and scientific research, many Americans embraced this promise and the seemingly miraculous hope it offered.

Formidable Challenges

The challenges facing embryonic stem cells were formidable. First, there was the concern that the cells and their derived tissue would be rejected by the patient's immune system, requiring the patient to undergo lifelong immune suppression. The three proposed solutions to this incompatibility problem (generating large banks of stem cell lines, cloning human embryos to provide a source of cells that perfectly match the patient, or genetically engineering stem cells to reduce immune rejection) were either socially, scientifically, or morally problematic (or all three). Second, there was the serious problem that embryonic stem cells form tumors when transplanted to adult tissues, and the tumorogenic capability of these cells is difficult, if not impossible, to control. Finally, there was the disturbing fact that science had thus far provided essentially no convincing evidence that embryonic stem cells could be reliably differentiated into normal adult cell types, as well as the disturbing possibility that overcoming this barrier would prove a difficult scientific endeavor.

Despite these concerns, many continued to regard embryonic stem cells with hope, believing that further research would overcome these difficulties and harness the power of embryonic stem cells for the benefit of mankind. Such optimists asserted that it was simply a matter of investing sufficient time, money, and research. . . .

Stem cell-based therapies propose to treat human medical conditions by replacing cells that have been lost through disease or injury. Unlike an organ transplant, where a damaged or diseased tissue is removed and then replaced with a comparable organ from a donor, stem cell therapies would involve integration of replacement cells into the existing tissues of the patient. The dispersed integration of the transplanted cells throughout the targeted organ (indeed, throughout the entire body of the patient) would make it impossible to remove the stem cell derivatives surgically should any problems arise. Thus, the problem of immune rejection is of particular concern—if transplanted cells are attacked by the immune system, the entire tissue in which the foreign cells reside becomes the target of a potentially disastrous immune attack.

Cloning Human Embryos

Over the past five years, the scientific community has focused almost exclusively on somatic-cell nuclear transfer, or cloning, as the best resolution to the problem of immune rejection. During somatic-cell nuclear transfer, the genetic information of an unfertilized human egg would be removed and replaced with the unique genetic information of a patient. This would produce a cloned, one-cell embryo that would mature for several days in the laboratory and then be destroyed to obtain stem cells genetically matched to the patient. Based on the success of animal cloning, human cloning was optimistically predicted to be a simple matter. Once we were able to clone human embryos, those embryos would provide patient-specific stem cell repair kits for anyone requiring cell-replacement therapies.

Human cloning has proved to be more challenging than anticipated. Human eggs, as it turns out, are considerably more fragile than eggs of other mammalian species, and they

Public Opinion on Embryonic Stem Cell Research

The Gallup Poll question: Please tell me whether you personally believe that in general it is morally acceptable or morally wrong to use stem cells obtained from human embryos.

	May 2002 (%) Embryo	May 2003 (%) Embryo
Morally acceptable	39	38
Morally wrong	52	54
No opinion	6	5
Depends on situation (volunteered)	2	3
Not a moral issue (volunteered)	1	NA
Total number polled	1,015	1,005

TAKEN FROM: Gallup Organization with CNN and *USA Today*, 2002/ 2003.

do not survive the procedures that were successfully used to clone animals. Multiple attempts by several research groups worldwide have been unsuccessful in generating human clones. The few reports of the successful cloning of human embryos were either unverifiable press releases or clear chicanery promoted by a quasi-religious group for its own publicity.

A Cloning Scandal

The elusive prize to generate the first human clone appeared to be won in March 2004, when a South Korean group led by Hwang Woo-Suk reported in the prestigious professional journal *Science* that they had generated a human stem cell line from a cloned human embryo. A year later, in June 2005, this same group sensationally reported that they had successfully generated eleven patient-specific stem cell lines from cloned human embryos and had dramatically improved their success rate to better than one in twenty attempts, bringing cloning into the realm of the possible for routine treatment of human medical conditions. Hwang was hailed as a hero and a pioneer, and his reported success evoked an almost immediate clamor to remove the funding restrictions imposed by the Bush administration on human embryonic stem cell research, lest America fall hopelessly behind South Korea in developing therapies.

By fall 2005, however, the cloning miracle had begun to unravel. Colleagues of Hwang raised serious concerns about his published studies, launching an investigation into possible scientific fraud. By December, it was conclusively shown that all the claimed cloned stem cell lines were fakes. To date, no one has successfully demonstrated that it is indeed possible to clone human embryos, and, based on the failed attempts of Hwang and others, human cloning is not likely to be a simple task, should it prove possible at all. . . .

Clones Are Not Normal

The technical challenges encountered by Hwang are not particularly surprising. Experience from multiple laboratories over the past decade confirms that it is extremely difficult to clone any animal. Cloned embryos are generally quite abnormal, with those that are sufficiently normal to survive to live birth typically representing between 0.1 and 2 percent. The problems do not end with the technical difficulty of somatic-cell nuclear transfer itself. Extensive evidence indicates that even the cloned animals that make it to birth are not untarnished success stories. Following Ian Wilmut's production of Dolly the sheep, the world's first cloned mammal, it was almost immediately evident that Dolly was not normal; she experienced a number of medical problems that resulted in her being euthanized, due to poor health, at the age of six years, about half the lifespan of a healthy sheep. Dolly was the only clone to survive to live birth out of the 277 cloned embryos Wilmut's group generated, yet this success did not prove that cloning can produce a normal sheep. Dolly was merely normal enough to survive birth.

In the past five years, a number of studies have carefully examined patterns of gene expression in mice and other cloned animals that survived to birth. Not one of these animals is genetically normal, and multiple genes are aberrantly expressed in multiple tissues. Both the severity and the extent of these genetic abnormalities came as a surprise to the cloning field, and yet, in retrospect, they are not surprising at all. The fact that most cloned embryos die at early stages of development is entirely consistent with the conclusion that somatic-cell nuclear transfer does not generate normal embryos, even in the rare cases where clones survive to birth. Thus, the optimistic contention that "therapeutic cloning" would fix the immune problem facing potential embryonic stem cell-based therapies for humans seems thus far entirely unsupported by the scientific evidence. . . .

The Problem of Tumors

It was unambiguously clear five years ago that embryonic stem cells robustly form tumors (teratomas) when transplanted into adult tissues, and this remains the case today. Teratomas are benign tumors that contain a variety of differentiated cell types (hair, teeth, muscle, etc.). These tumors can often prove fatal because of their rapid growth, but they are not malignant or cancerous tumors, which metastasize into multiple locations within the body. Embryonic stem cell advocates were well aware of the tumor-forming potential of these cells. (Indeed, teratoma formation following injection of embryonic stem cells into adult mice is still today the test of whether a researcher has successfully generated a bona fide embryonic stem cell line.) Embryonic stem cell advocates dismiss the threat of these tumors, however, claiming this would prove a problem only for undifferentiated embryonic stem cells.

These optimistic predictions have not held up to scientific experimentation. The tumor-forming potential of embryonic stem cells has proved a significant problem that does not show signs of being resolved any time soon. More than a dozen papers over the past five years (five papers within the past year alone) have shown tumor formation in animals treated with differentiated embryonic stem cell derivatives. In several of these studies, a shocking 70 to 100 percent of the experimental animals succumbed to fatal tumors. In all cases, tumors were believed to be derived from embryonic stem cells that either failed to differentiate or from cells that somehow de-differentiated once transplanted. Although experimental approaches designed to reduce tumor formation from differentiated embryonic stem cell derivatives are under investigation, it is not clear whether these approaches will ever prove successful, especially if the tumors are due to uncontrolled de-differentiation of the embryonic stem cell-derived tissues back to a more primitive state once they are transplanted to an adult environment.

From Benign to Malignant

Even more alarming than formation of benign (albeit, fatal) tumors, several studies over the past five years have raised concerns that the longer embryonic stem cells are maintained in the laboratory (or, presumably, in the tissues of adult human patients), the more likely they are to convert to malignant cancer cells. Embryonic stem cells spontaneously accumulate the genetic abnormalities associated with embryonal carcinoma (a form of testicular cancer). Embryonal carcinomas are believed to be the cancerous equivalent of embryonic stem cells and are a highly metastatic form of cancer. Although the finding that embryonic stem cells spontaneously convert to cancer cells over time remains contested, it is clear that some, if not all, embryonic stem cells undergo this conversion, and the factors controlling the transition are not well understood.

The assertion that embryonic stem cells in the laboratory can be induced to form all the cells comprising the mature human body has been repeated so often that it seems incontrovertibly true. What is missing from this assertion remains the simple fact that there is essentially no scientific evidence supporting it. Experiments have shown that embryonic stem cells are able to participate in normal embryonic development, an observation that is also true of cancerous embryonal carcinoma cells. When injected into early mouse embryos, both embryonic stem cells and embryonal carcinoma cells randomly contribute to every tissue of the developing body.

Questioning Therapeutic Potential

Even more dramatically, when embryonic stem cells are injected into mouse embryos under specific experimental circumstances (a procedure known as tetraploid complementation), they can be induced to form all the cells of the postnatal body. These experiments prove that embryonic stem cells (and embryonal carcinoma cells) remain capable of responding appropriately to the developmental signals that regulate tissue formation in the embryo, and from these results we can conclude that if embryonic stem cells were intended to provide cell replacement therapies for embryos, they would represent a very promising therapeutic approach. The problem, of course, is that embryos are not the intended targets of stem cell therapies, and there is little reason to believe that the capabilities of embryonic stem cells in an embryonic environment are relevant to their therapeutic potential for non-embryonic patients.

Five years ago, most scientists working in the field of embryonic stem cell research confidently predicted that we would soon determine the precise recipe of molecular factors required to replicate in the laboratory the mysterious inner life of the embryo. David Anderson, a stem cell researcher at Caltech, boldly asserted in a *New York Times* opinion piece that once science had figured out the factors required to repli-cate embryonic development, specific molecules could simply be "thrown into the bubbling cauldron of our petri dishes," where they would transform embryonic stem cells into an un-limited source of replacement cells for any tissue we chose to produce.

Skepticism regarding this claim was well warranted. While there have been hundreds of papers published over the past five years that stridently claim "cell type X produced from em-bryonic stem cells," under closer inspection these successes have all been less miraculous than they appeared. It is rela-tively easy to generate stem cell derivatives in the laboratory that have at least some of the properties of normal, mature cell types. But the test of whether an embryonic stem cell-derived brain cell, for example, is indeed a normal adult brain cell is to put it into the brain of an adult animal and deter-mine whether it survives and contributes to normal brain function. In addition, if laboratory-generated cells are to be therapeutically useful for the treatment of human disease and injury, they must be shown to have therapeutic value in adult animals: It is not sufficient that embryonic stem cell-derived cells merely survive in adults; they must also be able to repair the underlying disease or injury. It is precisely this kind of test that embryonic stem cell-derived tissues have proved unable to pass.

Transplant Failures

When cells derived from embryonic stem cells are transplanted into adult animals, their most common fate is to die. Indeed, most such transplanted tissue does not survive beyond a few weeks in an adult environment (the only exception is blood cells, where small numbers of cells survive long term in ma-ture animals). The rapid death of transplanted embryonic stem cell-derived cells stands in striking contrast to the robust survival of bona fide adult cells when transplanted to adult tissue. Typically, even the most promising experiments involving the transplant of embryonic stem cell derivatives have reported modest positive effects that persist for only a few weeks. In the few cases where tiny fractions of the transplanted cells survive for months (rather than weeks), this straggling band of survivors typically provides no therapeutic benefit.

The failure of embryonic stem cell-derived tissues to survive when transplanted to adult tissues strongly suggests that science has not yet determined how to generate normal adult tissue from embryonic stem cells. Why then do some studies show modest, short-term benefits from transplantation of such tissues? In many cases, the authors of these studies speculate that embryonic stem cell-derived transplants are not providing benefit because of replacement of lost or damaged cells but rather because the transplanted cells are supporting the survival or function of damaged adult tissues by secreting generic survival factors. Thus, the modest and transient benefits reported for embryonic stem cell-derived cell transplants over the past five years do not appear to require stem cells at all and are likely to be replicated by simply identifying the beneficial factors produced by the transplanted cells and supplying these factors directly.

"In light of the serious problems associated with embryonic stem cells," I noted in 2002, "there is no compelling scientific argument for the public support of research on human embryos." Serious scientific challenges are, by definition, problems that have stubbornly resisted the best attempts of science to resolve them. Over the past thirty years, hundreds of billions of dollars and countless hours of research by dedicated professionals worldwide have been devoted to solving the problems of immune rejection and tumor formation, yet these issues remain serious scientific and medical challenges. The mysteries of embryonic development have been plumbed for more than a hundred years by some of the most brilliant biologists of history, and yet, despite the clear progress we have made, we are nowhere near the point of having a "recipe book" for cooking up cellular repair kits to treat human disease and injury. Immune rejection, tumor formation, and embryonic development have proved themselves to be profoundly serious scientific challenges, and they are likely to remain so for decades into the future.

The hubris of scientists in the field of embryonic stem cell research who confidently asserted "Give us a few years of unrestricted funding and we will solve these serious scientific problems and deliver miraculous stem cell cures" was evident in 2002, and it is even more evident today. For the past five years, researchers have had completely unrestricted funding to conduct research on animal embryonic stem cells, and yet the serious scientific problems remain. They have had every conceivable tool of modern molecular research available to them for use in animal models, and yet the serious scientific problems remain. Millions of dollars have been consumed, and hundreds of scientific papers published, and yet the problems still remain. The promised miraculous cures have not materialized even for mice, much less for men.

Periodical Bibliography

The following articles have been selected to supplement the diverse views presented in this chapter.

Elizabeth Auster	"Legislators Must Remember History of Promising New Drugs," *Newhouse News Service*, March 13, 2007.
Joseph S. Bujak and Eric Lister	"Is the Science of Medicine Trumping the Art of Medicine?" *Physician Executive*, September/October 2006.
Richard Doerflinger	"Research Cloning and 'Fetus Farming': The Slippery Slope in Action," *United States Conference of Catholic Bishops Fact Sheet* May 2005.
Michael Gazzaniga	"All Clones Are Not the Same," *New York Times*, February 16, 2006.
Ellen Goodman	"A Dose of Reality on HPV Vaccine," *Boston Globe*, March 2, 2007.
Christine Gorman	"Are Doctors Just Playing Hunches?" *Time*, February 15, 2007.
Terrence P. Jeffrey	"Socializing Sexual Risk," *Townhall.com*, January 17, 2007.
Bill Maher	"Christians Crusade Against Cancer Vaccine," *Salon.com*, March 2, 2007.
Maryann Napoli	"New Cervical Cancer Vaccine Should Not Be Mandatory," *HealthFacts*, November 2006.
Neil Scolding	"Stem-Cell Therapy: Hope and Hype," *Lancet*, June 18, 2005.
Angela Shanahan	"Cloning by Any Other Name," *Quadrant*, October 2006.
Wesley J. Smith	"It Didn't Start with Dolly: Human Cloning Is Closer Than You Think," *Weekly Standard*, May 2, 2005.

OPPOSING
VIEWPOINTS®
SERIES

CHAPTER 4

What Is the Future of Medicine?

Chapter Preface

Every week, more than a hundred Americans who need transplants die before receiving them. In March 2007, more than ninety-five thousand people were on a national waiting list for organs. Indeed, the demand for organs has far exceeded the supply. While healthy people can donate their eyes, a few bones, a kidney, a portion of their skin or liver, and even a lung and still survive, few are willing to do so for a stranger. Growing desperation among activists, doctors, patients, and their families has renewed the debate over the ethics of organ sales. The sale of organs was banned in the United States as part of the National Organ Transplant Act of 1984. Organ sale activists claim, however, that legalizing organ sales would alleviate the shortage of transplantable organs by serving as an incentive to donate organs. While opponents raise several ethical concerns, the most common argument against organ sales is that such sales will exploit the poor.

Opponents argue that if organ sales were legal, those most likely to take the medical risk would be the desperately poor. "Letting people peddle their kidneys might save lives," argues science policy journalist Atul Gawande, "but the ethical price is too high." When people are desperate, these analysts assert, they are often unable to make well-reasoned decisions or effectively weigh the risks. "When an organ seller is trying to decide whether the terrible dangers from kidney removal or the certain loss of sight from surrendering an eye is worth a sudden cash infusion," Gawande claims, "his effort to identify his best interest will be confused by . . . difficulties sorting out the statistical risks, by the vision of all that money, and many other factors." Organ sale opponents also point out that society has traditionally outlawed other irrevocable options that are not in people's best interest. "In human experimentation," Gawande explains for example, "researchers cannot pay volunteers so much that the poor could be exploited. Rules limit how much blood you can donate or sell at one sitting. And while we allow people to give a kidney to their child, we do not allow them to donate their heart." For the same reasons, opponents argue, society is right to outlaw the sale of organs. "People can be weak," Gawande observes, "and money is all too often the way to their heart."

Those who support organ sales believe that, in a free society, people should be allowed to make their own choices, including the decision to sell their organs. In fact, supporters reason, prohibiting organ sales is what is truly unfair to the poor. The money poor people could earn from the sale of their organs could substantially improve their lives and the lives of their families. "Many people in backward countries who have to struggle to earn a few dollars a month could catapult themselves to Western living standards by selling a kidney, an organ which is not essential for health for most people," claims Rabbi Dr. Asher Meir. Indeed, he reasons, it might improve their health "since they could give up back-breaking labor and afford modern medical treatments." Moreover, supporters argue, the money paid for black-market organs is siphoned off by an army of middlemen. "This," Meir argues, "is truly a tragic exploitation of the poor."

Commentators continue to debate whether the future of transplant medicine lies in lifting the ban on organ sales. The authors in the following chapter debate other technologies and policies that they hope will improve the future of medicine.

> "[P]eople of faith already knew that you
> don't need a scientific study to prove
> that . . . prayer makes a difference."

Intercessory Prayer's Benefits Cannot Be Measured by Science

Tom Ryan

In the following viewpoint, Father Tom Ryan asserts that scientific studies that show no medicinal benefit from intercessory prayer do not prove that prayer has no healing power. Intercessory prayer, he argues, is a way for people to offer themselves as channels for God's healing powers. While the cures that science can measure may be what people want, God's healing power reflects His will, which may be a form of healing that does not result in a medical cure, Ryan claims. Ryan is director of the Paulist Office for Ecumenical and Interfaith Relations in New York.

As you read, consider the following questions:

1. According to Ryan, what did some scientists hope the results of a $2.5 million study of therapeutic prayer would bring?

2. What Biblical examples does the author provide as evidence that intercession makes a difference in what God finally does?

3. What form of intercession is the Lord's Prayer, in the author's opinion?

Scientists have been trying for at least a decade to determine whether organized prayer on the behalf of others can influence the outcome of medical treatment. Results from the largest study yet, released at the end of March [2006] on the therapeutic power of prayer by strangers, has found that it provided no benefit to the recovery of patients who had undergone cardiac bypass surgery.

Some scientists had hoped the results of the $2.5-million study, conducted at six U.S. medical centers, would bring an end to the long controversy over therapeutic prayer.

Some news commentators seemed pleased to announce that there was finally a formal debunking of the "magical expression" of religion that is intercessory prayer.

Biblical Stories of Intercession

These commentators seemed unfamiliar with the biblical stories. Stories that make it clear that we are in the presence of a God who works with us and for us to make and keep human life genuinely human, and whose ways are subject to change without notice. There are multiple illustrations in that unfolding story of how the intercessions of those who care make a difference in what God finally does.

To wit: in the book of Genesis, Abraham intercedes with God on behalf of the righteous in Sodom, extracting a promise that God will not sweep them away with the wicked.

In the book of Exodus, when God's anger burns hot against the people for worshipping a golden calf, Moses pleads on their behalf: "Turn from your fierce wrath: change your mind and do not bring disaster on your people" (32:11). The

---

Religion and Medicine

Americans who believe in the healing power of prayer	82%
Americans who believe God sometimes intervenes to cure serious illnesses	77%
Proven examples of spiritual healing, according to Christian Scientists	50,000
Christian Science church members	100,000–170,000
Chapter and verses in Leviticus that condemns taking of blood	17:10, 11
Child deaths linked to religion-based denial of health care (1975-1995)	172
Amount paid by federal government to Christian Science nursing homes since 1992	$50 million

TAKEN FROM: Issues and Controversies, "Religion and Medicine," June 18,1999.

---

account ends with "And the Lord changed his mind about the disaster that he planned to bring on his people."

These and other examples, like Jacob's wrestling with the angel until he received the desired blessing, have formed not only the religious imagination but also the religious practice of the children of Abraham for millennia. Underlying them is what scripture scholar Walter Wink has called "a mysterious law of the world of prayer," that God has somehow placed God's power in the hands of persons who intercede, in such a way that unless they intercede, that power is withheld.

Apparently, what God is looking for are active collaborators in causes that God wishes to espouse but has no desire to do alone. Take, for example, the only prayer that Jesus formally taught his followers. After the opening salutation of the Our Father, every phrase in the prayer is one of petition.

Intercession, according to the Lord's Prayer, is a prayer for God's reign to come on earth. That is to say, it is a prayer for the victory of God over disease, oppression, suffering and death in the concrete circumstances of people's lives here and now. Far from being an escape from action, it focuses for action. In our intercessions, we fix our wills on the divine possibility latent in the present moment and engage with God in the struggle to actualize it.

Praying for What God Wants

Some saw the study's results as proof [that] the God of the universe cannot be mechanically requisitioned to intervene in peoples suffering or health. That view of things, I would suggest, puts the cart before the horse by putting what we want first. Suppose that it is God who wants to intervene but will not do so without the expression of our love and care.

Suppose that we were to drop our presumption that we even know what a given individual really needs, and simply pray for what God wants, offering ourselves as channels of God's love and healing and leaving [the] results to God's wisdom.

Suppose that we were to give more place to the distinction between "curing" which relates to a physical condition, and "healing" which can take place on an emotional or spiritual level in the course of an illness even if the person dies.

Suppose we were to recognize that medical treatment itself could be a form of intercessory prayer.

As Dr. Herbert Benson, associate professor of medicine at Harvard Medical School and one of the study's lead researchers, said, "Nothing this study has produced should interfere with people praying for each other."

But people of faith already knew that you don't need a scientific study to prove that somehow, in God's mysterious economy, prayer makes a difference.

| "[D]istant prayer had absolutely no beneficial effect on any health outcomes."

Intercessory Prayer Has No Medicinal Benefits

Bruce L. Flamm

If intercessory prayer were a drug being tested by the FDA, asserts Bruce L. Flamm in the following viewpoint, it would not be approved. According to Flamm, a strict clinical study found that distant prayers had no beneficial effect on the health of cardiac bypass surgery patients. Since the prayer advocates who funded the study continue to believe in prayer's healing power, they probably did not expect these results, he reasons. Flamm is a clinical professor of obstetrics and gynecology at the University of California–Irvine.

As you read, consider the following questions:

1. How does Flamm distinguish bedside and distant prayer?
2. What anecdote does the author reveal about those patients who were told that they would receive distant prayers?

3. According to the author, what will be some of the excuses used to explain the failure of prayer?

For almost a decade, investigators at six academic medical centers including Harvard and the Mayo Clinic have been working on a major study of distant prayer. The results of their monumental effort, the largest study ever to search for effects of intercessory prayer, have now been published and the conclusion is crystal clear: prayer had no beneficial effects whatsoever.

The research, called the STEP trial (for "Study of the Therapeutic Effects of Intercessory Prayer") was meticulously designed to detect any effects of distant prayer. Note that prayer or loving words said at the bedside may reassure a patient and cause soothing physiologic mind/body interactions. In contrast, distant prayer is claimed to work via supernatural or paranormal mechanisms. This study was designed specifically to investigate distant prayer.

Studying Prayer

STEP investigators enrolled 1,802 cardiac bypass surgery patients from six hospitals and randomly assigned each to one of three groups: 604 patients received intercessory prayer after being informed they may or may not receive prayers (Group 1); 597 patients did not receive prayer after being informed they may or may not receive prayer (Group 2); and 601 patients received intercessory prayer after being informed they definitely would receive it (Group 3). The study enlisted members of three Christian groups, two Catholic and one Protestant, to provide prayer throughout the multiyear study.

To avoid bias and to ensure the results would be valid, none of the patients in the first two groups and none of their doctors knew which patients were being prayed for. This complex type of study, called a randomized double-blind controlled trial, is considered to be the gold standard for scientific proof.

Prayer and Healing Studies Are Mostly Unreliable

Most studies on whether prayer and religion can improve health are based on insufficient evidence, according to a recent evaluation of 150 studies. While evidence was found to be persuasive that people who go to church are healthier than non-churchgoers, evidence that religion hinders recovery from illness was found more credible than studies showing that religion improves recovery.

Hypothesis of study	Strength of evidence
Churchgoers are healthier than non-churchgoers	Persuasive
Religion or spirituality protects against cardio-vascular disease	Somewhat persuasive
Being prayed for improves physical recovery from acute illness	Somewhat persuasive
Religion or spirituality protects against cancer mortality	Inadequate
Religion or spirituality protects against disability	Inadequate
People who use religion to cope with difficulties live longer	Inadequate
Deeply religious people are protected against death	Consistent failures
Religion or spirituality slows the progression of cancer	Consistent failures
Religion or spirituality impedes recovery from acute illness	Somewhat persuasive
Religion or spirituality improves recovery from acute illness	Consistent failures

TAKEN FROM: Lynda Powell, et al., "Religion and Spirituality: Linkages to Physical Health," *American Psychologist*, January 2003.

What did they find? When the mountain of data was sub-
jected to statistical analysis the researchers found no signifi-

cant differences in any outcomes between groups 1 and 2. In other words, when patients did not know if they were being prayed for, distant prayer had absolutely no effect.

Interestingly, the patients who were told that they definitely would receive distant prayers (Group 3) actually had worse outcomes than the other two groups. Was this the work of an angry god? Probably not. The study authors postulated that telling patients they definitely would receive prayer may have increased their anxiety levels by leading them to believe that they were so sick that they needed prayer. The high anxiety and stress thus generated may have caused more complications, such as irregular heartbeats.

A Confusing Response

Bob Barth of Silent Unity, the prayer organization in Lee's Summit, Missouri, that was the Protestant group involved in the study, said the results didn't shake his confidence in prayer. "People of faith don't need a prayer study to know that prayer works," he said. Dozens of newspaper articles about the study included similar comments.

This raises an interesting question. Why waste several years and millions of dollars conducting a rigorous multicenter prayer study if you are not going to believe the results? Could it be that these were not the results that investigators were hoping for? Would they have questioned the results if prayer was found to be effective? The $2.5-million study was funded primarily by the John Templeton Foundation, an organization that pumps millions of dollars each year into efforts to promote religion and superstitious beliefs.

Father Dean Marek, a Catholic priest and co-principal investigator of Mayo's part of the STEP study opined, "I'm sure God will be very pleased with the results of this and getting people talking about the results of prayer in their lives." Since the study showed absolutely no beneficial effects of prayer one must wonder exactly what Father Marek has in mind. Perhaps he means that people should be talking about the fact that prayer is a waste of time.

More likely he is referring to the countless excuses that will be used to explain the complete failure of prayer in this major study. A few examples include: God knew it was a study so he did not answer the prayers; God does not like to be tested; God prefers prayers from family members; the prayers were answered but not the way we expected; and of course the classic, God works in mysterious ways. The truth is that once supernatural phenomena are claimed, the list of potential explanations for failure becomes infinite. In other words, for true believers the claimed healing effect of distant prayer is nonfalsifiable; nothing could ever change their minds.

A Fatal Blow

But for people who make decisions based on evidence, intercessory prayer has been dealt a fatal blow. The results of the STEP research confirm the results of the MANTRA II trial, another major study that was published [in 2005]. The MANTRA II study evaluated prayer in hundreds of cardiac patients at nine medical centers. Just like the STEP study, it concluded that distant prayer had absolutely no beneficial effect on any health outcomes.

Only one randomized controlled scientific study has ever demonstrated apparently profound effects of distant prayer. However, the Cha/Wirth/Lobo "Columbia Miracle Study" turned out to be highly flawed and almost certainly fraudulent. Co-author Daniel Wirth was convicted of criminal fraud and is now incarcerated in federal prison: co-author Rogerio Lobo of Columbia University has removed his name from the bizarre research.

In simple terms, the STEP and MANTRA II studies both found intercessory prayer to be totally worthless. If prayer was a drug being tested for effectiveness, these well-designed studies would have destroyed it. A medication that failed this miserably in two huge randomized trials would never be approved by the FDA [Food and Drug Administration].

> *"We must demystify genetic testing. It saves lives."*

Genetic Testing Will Save Lives

Albert de la Chapelle

According to Albert de la Chapelle in the following viewpoint, genetic testing for diseases that can be prevented or treated will save many lives. Like tests that show high cholesterol levels or high blood pressure, genetic tests give people an opportunity to come up with a life-saving medical treatment plan. People should be reassured that genetic tests are safe and that the results will not lead to discrimination against them, de la Chapelle asserts. De la Chapelle is professor of cancer genetics at the Ohio State University Comprehensive Cancer Center.

As you read, consider the following questions:

1. What syndrome is associated with the new mutation discovered by de la Chapelle and his colleagues?
2. Why in the author's view are some people afraid of knowing the outcome of genetic tests?
3. What in the author's opinion is a more important question than whether people should have genetic tests?

Earlier this year [2004], a group of Ohio State colleagues and I, collaborating with genetics researchers at Creighton University Medical Center in Omaha, Nebraska, discovered a new cancer-causing genetic mutation that proved to be a so-called founder mutation. A founder mutation is one that is brought into a population such as the United States by a single individual (in this case someone from Germany) and then spreads so that it becomes relatively common.

A Founder Mutation

The story is fascinating: The founder couple settled in Pennsylvania in 1727. They had 11 children, and the whereabouts of some of their descendants could be traced. Over the ensuing 13 generations, many descendants moved south and west, some as far as Texas and California.

Already more than 80 carriers of this mutation have been identified in 14 states. Researchers are eager to determine more precisely how common the mutation is.

Theoretically, if a person 13 generations ago had three children, and if in the ensuing generations all individuals had three children, the number of direct descendants would be greater than 1.5 million! Fortunately, the great majority of these descendants would not have the mutation.

The new mutation is one of many that cause a syndrome called hereditary nonpolyposis colorectal cancer, or Lynch syndrome, named after Dr. Henry Lynch at Creighton University. People with Lynch syndrome are strongly predisposed toward developing certain cancers. They have up to an 80 percent lifetime risk for colon cancer, and women have a 60 percent lifetime risk for uterine cancer. Other organs also are susceptible to cancer, but to a lesser degree.

People who carry Lynch syndrome mutations can greatly benefit from clinical surveillance for early signs of cancer. Regular colonoscopy can reduce their odds of dying from colon cancer by 60 percent or more.

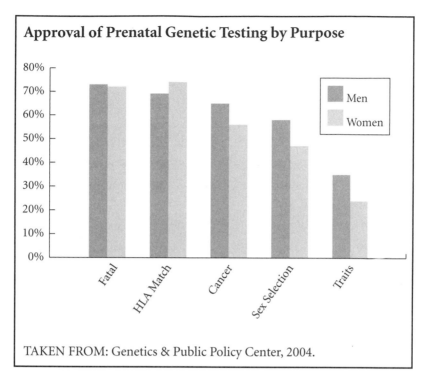

Approval of Prenatal Genetic Testing by Purpose

TAKEN FROM: Genetics & Public Policy Center, 2004.

Demystifying People's Fears

Detecting these mutations therefore saves lives. Yet, some people opt not to have genetic testing done. This is often a mistake. Some people are simply "afraid of knowing." They feel it would stigmatize their family if a disease-causing mutation were found. True, testing is possible for some diseases that can neither be treated nor prevented, such as Huntington's disease. To choose against being tested for one of these mutations may not be a bad decision.

But the situation is different for many cancers. People with a predisposing mutation usually can receive life-saving help. Thus, deciding against testing can be a grave mistake, a mistake that is compounded when it affects the individual's relatives, especially siblings and children, some of whom may have inherited the mutation.

Some people avoid genetic testing because they fear the results will make them uninsurable or raise their premiums. This may be true in some states, but I am optimistic that this country will soon follow several progressive European countries in outlawing insurance discrimination based on genetic test results.

Some individuals believe genetic testing interferes with their genes or heritage, or the genes of their descendants. Such fears are unwarranted. Genetic tests are safe and require no more than a blood sample.

Genetic tests like those for Lynch syndrome signal a high likelihood of disease, as do findings such as elevated blood sugar or a narrowed brain artery. Yet, those tests are ordered without hesitation.

Other genetic tests signal a moderately greater risk for cancer. Similarly, tests showing high cholesterol, high blood pressure, or overweight also predict moderately elevated risks for disease. An X-ray showing an enlarged heart often tells more about a patient's life-expectancy than any genetic test.

A more important question is who should be tested. Lynch syndrome accounts for less than 5 percent of all colorectal and endometrial cancers, so it would be a huge waste of resources to test all patients with these diseases. Nor should we test all descendants of early 18th century German immigrants or those with ancestors in Pennsylvania.

Lynch syndrome runs in families, so members of families with a history of colon and uterine cancer should consider genetic testing. So should people who develop these cancers early, before age 50. Certain characteristics of the tumor itself also can flag a person with Lynch syndrome.

People seeking genetic testing should meet with a professional, a clinical geneticist or a genetic counselor, preferably at an academic medical center.

This is essential. Experienced counselors will help patients avoid unnecessary tests, provide the most accurate interpretation of test results and outline the best medical follow-up plan. We must demystify genetic testing. It saves lives.

| "*Fears [of genetic discrimination] may be deadly if they prevent people who are at risk from undergoing genetic testing . . .*"

Genetic Testing Could Lead to Discrimination

Henry T. Greeley

Legislation banning discrimination based on genetic testing is necessary, maintains Henry T. Greeley in the following viewpoint. Genetic discrimination bans will allay public fears that might otherwise prevent at-risk people from getting life-saving tests. In addition, Greeley claims, genetic information bans will assuage fears that prevent people from participating in research that could lead to advances in medicine. A ban would also protect Americans from irrational insurers and employers. Greeley is a professor of law and genetics at Stanford University.

As you read, consider the following questions:

1. What three factors explain the absence of genetic discrimination in health coverage and employment, in Greeley's view?

2. According to the author, why is educating the public about the small risk of discrimination not enough?

Henry T. Greeley, "Banning Genetic Discrimination," *New England Journal of Medicine*, vol. 353, September 1, 2005, pp. 865–67. Reproduced by permission.

3. What does the author claim will be some of the costs of genetic discrimination legislation?

Americans have been haunted by the fear of genetic discrimination since the beginnings of genetic testing more than 30 years ago. The launch of the Human Genome Project in 1990, however, brought a whole new level of scrutiny and sophistication to the consideration of genetic information. In general, the fear has focused on health insurance, since insurers have an incentive to identify and avoid clients who will cost them more money than the average client. Similar incentives apply to employers, who not only are concerned about the effects of employees' health problems on productivity but also pay for most private health care in the United States.

Published accounts of reported genetic discrimination in both life insurance and employment surfaced in the 1990s,[1] along with an increasing number of policy recommendations expressing concern about the potential for genetic discrimination and arguing for legislation against it.[2;3] However, the early reports often involved allegations of discrimination on the basis of disease, rather than a genetic predisposition to disease. Subsequent studies have shown that although there is widespread concern about genetic discrimination, there are few examples of it—and no evidence that it is common.[4]

In retrospect, this finding is not surprising. A simple model would predict that a rational insurer or employer would discriminate on the basis of genetic information if the savings that could be expected from doing so outweighed the costs—in litigation, in employee satisfaction, in public relations, and in sheer administrative outlays. For the savings to be substantial, the genetic test would have to have strong predictive power, the costs associated with the genetic condition would have to be high, and the probability that it would occur while the person was covered by the insurer or employer would also have to be high. The apparent absence of genetic discrimination in health coverage and employment is probably the result of three factors: the structure of the health care financing system, state and federal legislation, and the limits of recent progress in human genetics.

Few Americans have health coverage from organizations that pick and choose whom to cover on the basis of health, using what is called medical underwriting. More than 160 million Americans receive coverage through an employer, whether their own, their spouse's or partner's, or that of another relative. Few large-scale employers ever selectively provided health coverage on the basis of an employee's medical condition; the federal Health Insurance Portability and Accountability Act of 1996 prohibited almost all employers but those in the smallest businesses from using such medical underwriting and from considering genetic risks as preexisting conditions. More than 80 million Americans are covered by federal or federal-state programs—notably, Medicare and Medicaid—that do not use medical underwriting. Very few of the more than 40 million Americans without health coverage lack it because of genetic discrimination; most simply do not qualify for governmental coverage and either cannot afford or choose not to pay for employer-provided or individually underwritten coverage. That leaves only about 10 to 15 million Americans who buy their own, individually underwritten coverage, along with perhaps an equal number with coverage from very small employers. Only the people in these two groups can be at risk for genetic discrimination by insurance companies. But the same health care financing system that limits the possibilities for genetic discrimination by insurers encourages such discrimination in employment. Employers have an incentive to reduce their future health insurance costs by not hiring or by firing people who have predictably high health care expenses, for genetic or other reasons.

The law provides a second barrier against genetic discrimination. In the past decade or so, all but 3 states have adopted laws limiting genetic discrimination for some kinds of health

Barriers to Effective Care

At the National Institutes of Health, study volunteers are hesitant to participate in critical biomedical research because they are concerned that their genetic information will not be kept confidential and will be used by health insurers or employers to discriminate against them. Individuals in a preliminary NIH colon cancer study were provided education and counseling before being offered the genetic test. In response to being asked what factors might lead them to take the test, the overwhelming majority stated that they wished to learn about their children's health risks and to gain information to help them plan their own cancer screening.

When asked what factors might lead them not to take the test, the primary concern cited by 39% was losing insurance. In a similar study involving genetic testing for increased risk of breast and ovarian cancer, fully one third of the individuals who chose not to participate did so because of their concern about genetic discrimination. As the applications of genetics move out of the research lab and into broad clinical practice, this problem will only become more acute.

Bobby P. Jindal, "Protecting Against Genetic Discrimination: The Limits of Existing Laws," Testimony, Committee on Health, Education, Labor and Pensions Hearing, United States Senate, Washington, DC, February 13, 2002.

insurance, and about 40 states have fairly strong rules against discrimination by small employers or companies that sell individual health insurance. More than 30 states ban or limit genetic discrimination in employment.[5] The coverage, definitions, and enforcement mechanisms vary enormously from state to state; none of the relevant laws appear to have been defined or tested in any reported appellate-court decisions. In addition, the federal Americans with Disabilities Act, passed in 1990, may more broadly prohibit genetic discrimination in employment, depending on whether the genetic risk is considered a disability. Another federal law, the Employee Retirement Income Security Act, prohibits an employer from discriminating against current employees on the basis of their existing or projected health care expenses. Although the exact reach of these federal laws is unclear, they—along with state laws and the prospect of more stringent legislation in the future—have largely deterred insurers and employers from practicing such discrimination.

In the wake of the Human Genome Project, the third factor may strike some as surprising, but in fact there have been few recent discoveries that lend themselves to abuse in the form of genetic discrimination. Deadly, dramatic, and highly penetrant genetic diseases were identified first because they were so obvious. Fortunately (and not surprisingly, from an evolutionary perspective), such diseases are uncommon. Although many common disorders, such as asthma, type 2 diabetes mellitus, coronary artery disease, and schizophrenia, seem to have some genetic component, understanding the genetic contribution has proved to be difficult. And if a person's genetic variations contribute only a small amount to his or her risk of disease—changing it, for example, from an 8 percent lifetime risk to 12 percent or 4 percent—this genetic information will be too weak to prompt discrimination. The extent to which genetic contributions to common diseases will lead to strong or weak predictions of future illness remains uncertain.

Although actual genetic discrimination may not be a substantial reality, several factors argue for enacting laws against it. Even if only a small fraction of the population may be at high genetic risk for serious illness and therefore for genetic discrimination that could be thought of as "rational," protecting such people may be worthwhile. Moreover, employers and insurers sometimes act foolishly: they may discriminate in ways that are irrational but that nonetheless harm people. Perhaps most important, regardless of how likely genetic discrimination may be, the fear of it is quite real. Such fears may be deadly if they prevent people who are at risk from undergoing genetic testing, and they may have broader ill effects if they keep people from participating in research that could lead to medical advances.

If unreasonable fear were the only problem, one solution might be to educate the public about the small size of the actual risks. But current protections against genetic discrimination are complicated, confusing, and uncertain. A broad but careful federal law against such discrimination could provide reassurance that no combination of rational arguments and state laws can offer.

Of course, all legislation has costs. Any definition of "genetic information" might end up being too broad or too narrow. Any new basis for appropriate lawsuits will inevitably provide the basis for some inappropriate claims. And the mere fact that Congress has passed legislation against genetic discrimination might have the perverse effect of convincing the public that the risk of discrimination is actually high. But although the Genetic Information Nondiscrimination Act is not perfect, the Senate has unanimously concluded correctly that it is an important step forward.

A wide range of organizations have joined the White House in supporting the bill. And as the proposed legislation has evolved over the past decade, insurers have come to tolerate it, if not to welcome it. The main opposition now comes from employer groups such as the U.S. Chamber of Commerce, and even their objections focus on details of the legislation.

If the bill gets to the floor of the House of Representatives, it seems likely to be approved. But there is no guarantee that it will reach the floor. The House bill has been referred to three different committees; at least two of the relevant chairs have already expressed doubts about it. But the bill should be passed. Although it is not a panacea, the Genetic Information Nondiscrimination Act would be good for medicine, for science, and for the nation.

Endnotes

1. Billings PR, Kohn MA, deCuevas M, Beckwith J, Alper JS, Natowicz MR. Genetic discrimination as a consequence of genetic testing. Am J Hum Genet 1992;50:476–482.

2. Rothenberg KH, Fuller B, Rothstein M, et al. Genetic information and the workplace: legislative approaches and policy challenges. Science 1997;275:1755–1757.

3. Greely HT. Genotype discrimination: the complex case for some legislative protection. Univ PA Law Rev 2001;149:1483-1505.

4. Hall MA, Rich SS. Laws restricting health insurers' use of genetic information: impact on genetic discrimination. Am J Hum Genet 2000;66:293–307.

5. National Conference of State Legislatures. Genetics laws and legislative activity. (Accessed August 11, 2005, at http://www.ncsl.org/programs/health/genetics/ charts.htm.)

| "If we limit ourselves . . . we will rob ourselves and our descendants of some of the most exciting opportunities that the biological revolution presents."

Biological and Genetic Human Enhancement Will Improve Human Life

Arthur Caplan

Efforts to enhance human life are what makes people human, argues Arthur Caplan in the following viewpoint. The desire to improve ourselves through engineering is not vain; it is human nature. Humans, Caplan maintains, have evolved to adapt to their environment. Moreover, the genetic lottery already makes some people better at some things than others—not all improvements can be earned. Arguments that engineered enhancements will not be equitably distributed question human attitudes toward equality, not the value of human enhancement itself, he reasons. Caplan is director of the Center for Bioethics at the University of Pennsylvania.

Arthur Caplan, from *Better Humans? The Politics of Human Enhancement and Life Extension*, London: Demos, 2006, pp. 31–39. Copyright © Demos. Reproduced by permission.

As you read, consider the following questions:
1. What example of human enhancement does Caplan give to preview the challenges against enhancement?
2. What reasons other than vanity does the author suggest a person might have for looking better?
3. What does the author think is worse than claims human enhancement will be inequitable?

If I go to the laser surgery place and have my eyes tweaked, and I come out with better than what the limits of biology designed into me, 20/20 vision if I was lucky, am I committing a moral wrong? Am I vain? Is it inequitable because other people don't get their eyeballs done or couldn't afford it?

Is it something that we have to say is inauthentic? I didn't really earn it. I guess I didn't exercise my eyes. I didn't try to avoid staring too much at a computer screen. I didn't do the things that might have helped my vision along. I just lay down, the laser did its thing and my eyes are seeing better than ever.

And going even further, is it a distortion of who we are? If all of us run around with 20/15 vision, are we less than human? Have we become some sort of bizarre, unrecognisable, different type of being, disconnected from who we are today, unrecognisable to our forbears because we see better than any of them ever could have? . . .

The Quest for Perfection?

One of the things that's a little unfair about arguments [against human enhancement] is that most of the critics are saying, 'You shouldn't pursue perfection.' But, as [artist] Salvador Dali said, 'You don't have to worry about perfection; you're not going to get there.' What we're talking about is something different, something more interesting, but it's a little less spooky and that is improvement. 'Should we improve human nature?' is really the question. Not, 'Should we pursue perfection?' I think that rhetoric is an easy mark, an easy point of attack but I want to get it out of the way.

What the anti-meliorists, the anti-improvement people, are trying to argue is, 'Let's not head down the melioristic road.' And they look around and they say, 'You know what's going on right now? Breasts are being augmented. Wrinkles are being smoothed out. Fat is being suctioned out. Blood is being doped and moods are being calmed. If we don't put a stop to this, who knows where we're going to be? Everybody's going to have a breast job. Everybody's going to have pectoral implants. Everybody will run around trying to take drugs to alter their moods—to make them happy or complacent. We have to get on top of this push within the bioengineering side of things to try to change us because it's going to lead to places that we would find unappealing.'

Improvement and Vanity

The critics of human enhancement bring forward the argument that, 'If you want to look better, you're vain.' I would have thought, 'If you want to look better, you might say you have self-regard.' You might say that you are trying, in some sense, to present yourself in the world in a way that makes you feel better. You might say that it shows an appropriate level of interest in how others see you. You might even say, if you were sociobiological about it, that it might give you an advantage in the mating game.

But it doesn't just have to be a matter of vanity. If it's really all vain, then why don't we just take off our clothes, throw away the makeup, get rid of the fashion industry and reconcile ourselves to grubbing around in some sort of grass skirt and be done with it? We know that, to some extent, part of what gives us pleasure is trying to control our appearance, control how others see us. It may or may not be something that we can overindulge. I would grant that the person who undergoes perhaps their twentieth cosmetic surgery operation may be abusing the idea of biological change. But that doesn't show that it's always wrong if you don't like the shape of your nose, if you want to remove a port wine stain from your face, if you want to see better through laser surgery, if you'd prefer to wear contacts rather than glasses, if you even want to remove wrinkles. I don't find anything inherently and obviously and self-evidently wrong about this. . . .

I'm not arguing that it's right for 14-year-olds to get breast augmentation surgery as a gift, which some have. I think you should learn to decide whether you like your body or not and you're not ready at that age to make such a decision. But again, I'm going to say it's not self-evident to me that all pursuit of beauty or looks or appearance is vain, in and of itself. And certainly vanity has nothing to do with interest in trying to think faster, have more memory, or in the decision about whether one wants to be stronger or to be able to increase aptitudes and capabilities. That's not vanity; that's function.

Equity and Fairness

It is true that we could find ourselves, in the developed world, having access to genetic engineering, biological engineering, brain implants, biochemical interventions that poor people in other places cannot get. It's also true that we could find ourselves, within rich countries, with a lot of people unable to buy or purchase many of these things that might enhance or improve capacity.

But I have a very simple question. Is the problem modifying and improving our biological nature? Or is it a problem of inequity?

I'm not in favour of inequity. But, if I said, 'We're going to guarantee access to anyone who wants it to a chip that might be put into somebody's head and improve their memory,' and if I took equity off the table, there's no argument here other than it's bad to have inequity. Inequity is bad. But it's not connected necessarily to biological changes. It's connected to all sorts of important resources.

We already have a two-class system. I don't celebrate it. I don't endorse it. I think those inequities are wrong. But what's wrong is the inequities. It's not that they're biological. Any inequity that leads to these kinds of different abilities to enjoy and pursue life ought to be redressed. So what the inequity criticism misses is that what's wrong is inequity, not biology.

And worse, those people who keep telling us that they care about it so much do nothing to suggest rectification of environmental, social and familial inequity. They have nothing to say. It's only if I put a chip in my head. I can attend Harvard all day, apparently, and come up with the $40,000 it takes to go there and they don't care. But if it's some kind of intervention that might be biochemical, or bioengineered, that, for some reason, is a different kind of inequity and they don't like that.

That is not treating like cases alike; that's an old principle of morals. And I think the argument falls down here completely. Inequity is the problem, not biological engineering.

Satisfaction Guaranteed?

Well, what about this whole idea that it is wrong, that we will find ourselves unhappy, dispirited and dissatisfied if we have cheap victories? If we wind up using biological knowledge to engineer ourselves so that we can think more quickly in solving a problem, have more memory, figure out problems better than we could before because we've taken a drug? What if drugs out now like modafinil (Provigil) allow us to sleep less?

If we swallow a cup of coffee every morning and use that stimulant, should we all feel morally bad for a while? I mean, that's what the argument is. You're making a pharmacological intervention to get your attention going. And apparently, that's a cheap thrill that you don't really deserve. You should just

A Moral Imperative

We have a moral imperative to attempt to enhance ourselves and our children. . . . Choosing not to enhance someone is the same as harming them. All of us, I think, would accept that dietary neglect that caused a child with a stunning intellect to be stunted and have a normal intellect would be wrong, and a form of parental abuse. But failing to institute some diet that would cause a normal child to have a stunning intellect results in exactly the same thing: a child who's normal, who could have been much brighter, I believe is equally wrong. Now substitute "biological intervention" for "diet", and you see that if we have a reason to prevent our children from deteriorating we also have a reason to improve them.

Julian Savulescu, "National Australia Bank Address,"
speech, National Press Club, June 8, 2005.

wake your own damn self up and run around the block a few times rather than having these shortcuts.

Some people do think that the only way to get to the top of the mountain is to hike up there. I don't have a problem with that. If they like doing that, that's fine. Me, I like a helicopter. View's the same. I don't care. I get to the top. I get to see it. It's faster. I leave. . . .

There are plenty of things that you and I are all happy about that we have nothing to do with, that we don't struggle, practise, earn, fight for or do anything to attain. They just happen and we say, 'Well, that's good fortune.' Part of that, obviously, is a lesson of Darwinism.

I'm tempted to say, 'Stuff happens.' But there's a lot of stuff out there, the genetic lottery, so that you might say, 'Boy, I'm glad I can sing. Or I'm glad that I have good pitch. Or I'm really lucky that I have good hand—eye coordination.' I'm describing a number of things I don't have and I'm envious of. But I don't begrudge them. That's just how it is. You're lucky to have those things, and so that's nice. And I'm happy. And you're happy. And we don't sit around saying it's only earned happiness is the authentic happiness. I don't buy that argument at all. I think it's a distortion, in fact, of what makes human beings satisfied.

Creatures in Flux

So what remains in our march against the anti-meliorist here is this human nature argument. At bottom, the other ones, I think, collapse. They're not good arguments about why we shouldn't try to improve ourselves. Human nature is probably the last bastion of defence for the anti-meliorists.

We're a jumble of traits, behaviours, aptitudes, interests, capacities and volitions shaped by a set of historical accidents. The problem is that certain conservatives who would like to anchor the world keep trying to resurrect Platonic essentialism. In fact, the real worry for Darwinism isn't the scientific creationists, isn't the anti-evolutionists. They're just people who want religion introduced into people's lives.

The real threat is the anti-meliorists. Those who argue for a distinct essence, a kind of template of humanity that somehow is in there as a core that cannot be touched or changed or manipulated without loss of who we are—they are nervous conservatives who worry that the bearings will be lost if we admit that what we are is a jumbled set of mishmash traits evolved and designed to handle a random environment from the past that we don't have to care about any more.

The anti-meliorists don't tell us what human nature is. They posit a static notion of human nature which isn't consistent with evolution. They posit the view that what our nature is, whatever it is, is right, when we know that it's right only in relation to a set of environmental challenges that don't exist any more or that we're modifying all the time.

An Interesting Accident

We are a creature or species, as all are, in a state of flux. The anti-meliorists are making the conceptual error, that the way we are is the way we should be. I'm submitting that what we know from evolution, from Darwin's day on, is that the way we are is an interesting accident. And it tells us certain things about what will make us function well, but it doesn't tell us anything about the way we should be or what we should become or how we should decide to change ourselves.

I find no in-principle arguments why we shouldn't try to improve ourselves at all. I don't find it persuasive that to say you want to be stronger, faster, smarter makes you vain. Try to improve yourself. From Ben Franklin on, there are both secular and religious thinkers who urge improvement on our species and our individual selves.

That's what agriculture is. That's what plumbing is. That's what clothes are. That's what transportation systems are. They are all attempts by us to transcend our nature. Do they make us less human? Or are they the one possible contender for what it means to be human? This idea that we want to try and press change, improve. Maybe that's it. If that's it, I'll accept that because I think that may be the only thing we can draw out of evolution.

If we limit ourselves, in the way that many anti-meliorists are suggesting we do now, then we will rob ourselves and our descendants of some of the most exciting opportunities that the biological revolution presents.

> "[T]inkering with human qualities does not—cannot—lead to a transcendence of the human, only an amplification."

The Impact of Human Enhancement Is Uncertain

Bryan Appleyard

Human enhancement does not mean humans will become better, claims Bryan Appleyard in the following viewpoint. Human enhancement means that humans will be more human, and unfortunately, human nature is not always benign, he argues. Human progress has sometimes had tragic consequences, and people continue to engage in war, genocide, and torture. While society can decide to only make positive human enhancements, people will forever disagree over what those will be, he maintains. Appleyard, a British journalist, is author of How to Live Forever or Die Trying: On the New Immortality.

As you read, consider the following questions:

1. In Appleyard's view, what are some of the first steps being taken toward a program of human enhancement?

2. In what way does the author believe the definition of disease has been expanded?

Bryan Appleyard, "Design Fault," *Spectator*, March 4, 2006, p. 28. www.spectator .co.uk. Copyright © 2006 by *The Spectator*. Reproduced by permission of *The Spectator*.

3. In the author's opinion, from what do transhumanist dreamers suffer?

'Designer babies' is headline shorthand for a weird new world of genetic enhancement. Thanks to several generations of science-fiction imagery, it evokes an unnatural and evil world of blond, staring, probably homicidal children, which scares ordinary people.

Headlines create a cartoon world that subverts understanding and wisdom, but there is some truth in them. Human 'enhancement' is now being pursued in many ways, through life extension, psychoactive drugs like Ritalin and Prozac, information technology and, most obviously, through control of reproduction. The decoding of the human genome in 2000 signalled the start of an era in which we could hope to cure hitherto intractable diseases. But it also offers the chance to improve ourselves, to go for what the American techno-prophet Ray Kurzweil calls 'Human Body Version 2.0'.

Controlling Reproduction

The first steps towards a programme of human enhancement will be taken—are being taken—through control of reproduction. Pre-implantation genetic diagnosis (PGD) already allows us to weed out potentially diseased embryos. As our genome-reading tools become more accurate, it will also allow us to detect undesirable traits and select desirable ones. Further advances may well give us the option of manipulating the DNA of foetuses or, indeed, children.

Many detailed debates arise. For example, what is a cure and what is an enhancement? Is being short a condition that requires a cure? Is having below-average intelligence? In practice, however, these are distractions, for the simple reason that it will be impossible to draw a clear line between medical interventions and enhancements.

A great deal of disease is culturally (not scientifically) defined. The history of multiple personality disorder—superbly documented in Ian Hacking's book *Rewriting the Soul*—demonstrates that people's disquiet will manifest itself in the symptoms offered by the age. Furthermore, we now go to great lengths to console ourselves that conditions like alcoholism are diseases. This is not a clinical finding; it is an expansion of the definition of disease. Any such expansion is obviously limitless (I can think of many shortcomings of my own which it would be nice to regard as diseases) and, therefore, any attempt to hold an ethical line against enhancement is doomed to failure.

The Human Enhancement Debate

In fact, the real debate is much simpler, as a recent Demos essay collection—*Better Humans? The Politics of Human Enhancement and Life Extension*—makes clear. Essentially, this is the debate between those who think we can and/or must fundamentally improve the human condition and those who think we can't and/or shouldn't.

The concept of human nature is the issue. Genetic conservatives like Francis Fukuyama and Leon Kass argue that there is such a thing as human nature and that these new technologies threaten to change it. This would be disastrous as human nature is all we have and it has taken us this far. Fukuyama's celebrated 'end of history' argument—that the world is moving towards a final political condition of liberal democracy—is clearly dependent on the belief that this final condition is in accord with human nature. Radicals like Kurzweil, the bioethicist Arthur Caplan and the Oxford philosopher Nick Bostrom believe in the transcendence of the merely human, and that if there is such a thing as human nature, then its essence is precisely to pursue such transcendence, to become better than nature intended.

Two points need to be made about this confrontation. First, it depends on the conviction that these new technologies, notably of reproductive control, do represent a funda-

mental change in our capabilities. They are quite different from, say, antibiotics and surgery in that they appear to intervene in our innermost being, in what we usually call our souls. Some radicals deny this, arguing that there is an unbroken continuity between conventional medicine—and, indeed, public health measures and education—and the kind of enhancements now on offer. Furthermore, have not parents always wanted the best for their children? Are we now to tell them they cannot have it? But, of course, merely to argue that there is such a continuity cannot be to argue that it should be pursued at any cost. The continuity argument is, therefore, immaterial, rhetorical rather than rational. Continuity or not, there is what physicists would call a 'phase transition' happening in our capabilities, and that is what is being addressed.

Second, both conservatives and radicals are arguing from faith-based positions. The genetically conservative faith is in human nature, that it is real and, ultimately, benign. The radical faith is in progress and the future, that technological progress can be pursued into the depths of the human realm, that we can solve our inner problems as successfully as we have solved our outer ones. There is no real evidence for either of these positions; none, at least, strong enough to sway an honest sceptic.

Evidence of Human Failure

There is, however, evidence for human failure. The benignity of human nature is, in the light of our continuing propensity for war, genocide and mutual loathing, a dubious proposition. Equally dubious is the belief in progress in the light of our newly rediscovered enthusiasm for torture and for the continuing ingenuity with which we deploy new technologies to kill each other. Ethical progress plainly does not occur and, given the reality of anthropogenic global warming, material progress may soon prove to be catastrophic.

Ah, but, say the radicals, we can fix that by meddling with our DNA or whatever, we can design nice babies. But how? The idea of human enhancement is irrational for the simple reason that we cannot know what an enhancement would be. Crudely put, is it better to have a child who is Bill Gates or Mother Teresa, Albert Einstein or Albert Schweitzer? Though I don't doubt that it is better for the me that I have become that I was not born blind, does that make me better than a blind person?

Unanalysed Faith in the Superhuman

We have no standard by which to judge humans apart from other humans. The true metaphysic of the radical position is the absolutely unanalysed faith in the superhuman. Of course, there are many ideas of what a superhuman would be, but they don't all converge on the model of the Silicon Valley geeks who seem to be the most avid of transhumanist dreamers. All superhumanisms are tribal. A Palestinian superhuman would be very different from an Israeli. The geeks are, in the words of the sociologist Dan Sarewitz, suffering from 'conceptual cluelessness', because they don't see that tinkering with human qualities does not—cannot—lead to a transcendence of the human, only an amplification. Designing babies to be 'better' means designing them to be more, not less, like us.

The rational, evidence-based position is, therefore, pessimistic genetic conservatism. Technology amplifies human vices as surely as it does their virtues. Yet technology just seems to go on regardless. Whatever qualms we might have are crushed by its persuasive powers. We will, therefore, design our babies. They will certainly be no better than us and, with luck, no worse. The best we can hope for is that, having designed them, we can still find it in our hearts to love them. But that, I think, may turn out to be the real problem.

Periodical Bibliography

The following articles have been selected to supplement the diverse views presented in this chapter.

Ronald Bailey	"The Genetic Insurance Racket," *Reason*, February 23, 2005.
Lynne Brown	"Practiced by Millions, Prayer Is Worthy of More Study," *Alternative Therapies*, November/ December 2006.
Haley Casey and Nicholas Cram	"How the Internet Has Changed Modern Medicine," *Journal of Clinical Engineering*, April–June 2005.
Chicago Times	"Your Genetic 'Wellness Check,'" August 9, 2006.
Bette-Jane Crigger	"E-medicine: Policy to Shape the Future of Health Care," *Hastings Center Report*, January/ February 2006.
Madeline Drexler	"Your Genetic Test Is in the Mail," *Good Housekeeping*, May 2006.
Denise Grady	"Second Opinion: Genetic Test for Diabetes May Gauge Risk, But Is the Risk Worth Knowing?" *New York Times*, August 8, 2006.
Patrick J. Morrison	"Insurance, Unfair Discrimination, and Genetic Testing," *Lancet*, September 10, 2005.
Erik Ness	"Faith Healing," *Prevention*, December 2005.
Julia Neuberger	"Should We Choose Our Children?" *Lancet*, April 15, 2006.
Richard P. Sloan and Rajasekhar Ramakrishnan	"Science, Medicine, and Intercessory Prayer," *Perspectives in Biology and Medicine*, Autumn 2006.
Patrick Tucker	"Designer Babies and 21st Century Cures," *Futurist*, September/October 2006.

For Further Discussion

Chapter 1

1. Kai Wright contends that racism persists in medicine. In the past, people blamed biology for racial disparities in medical care. Today, those who refute claims of racism blame minority culture instead, he claims. Do you think the evidence Sally Satel provides to support her argument that doctors are not racist, blames minority culture for disparities in medical care? Explain why or why not, citing from both texts.

2. Sasha Polakow-Suransky claims that high jury awards improve medicine by deterring bad doctors. Sherman Joyce argues, on the other hand, that high jury awards do not act as a deterrent. Identify the types of evidence each author uses to support their claims. Which type of evidence do you find more persuasive? Explain, citing from the viewpoints.

3. Adam P. Summers argues that universal health care will increase the cost of medical care in the United States. Barack Obama maintains that the failure to provide health coverage for all Americans is more costly. What rhetorical strategies does each author use to support his claim? Which strategy do you believe is more persuasive? Explain, citing from the viewpoints.

4. Journalists Anne Hull and Dana Priest claim that U.S. soldiers are receiving substandard medical care. The editors of the *Economist* do not dispute this claim, arguing instead that the problem can be explained by the unpredictability of war. What evidence do the editors of the *Economist* provide to support their claim? Do you think this

evidence adequately addresses the concerns raised by Hull and Priest? Explain why or why not, citing from the viewpoints.

Chapter 2

1. Clare Bowerman claims that many alternative therapies are dangerous. Kristin Kane and Sharon Liao counter that many alternative therapies are safe and effective. What commonalities can you find in the types of evidence and rhetorical strategies the authors use to support their claims? How do their strategies differ? Which strategies do you believe are most persuasive? Citing from the viewpoints, explain.

2. Robert Ullman and Judyth Reichenberg-Ullman, who assert that homeopathy is effective medicine, admit that the reasons for homeopathy's success remain unknown. Edzard Ernst believes that homeopathy is not effective medicine and suggests that the homeopath's intimate interaction with the patient may explain homeopathy's effectiveness in individual cases. In your opinion, does Ernst's explanation adequately refute the Ullmans' claims? Explain why or why not, citing from the viewpoints?

3. Lester Grinspoon argues that medical marijuana is effective medicine and that bans should be removed. Andrea Barthwell claims that there is no evidence that smoked marijuana is good medicine and that bans are therefore necessary. Note each author's affiliation. Does this affiliation make his/her viewpoint more or less persuasive? Explain.

4. What commonalities among the evidence and rhetoric can you find in the viewpoints on both sides of the debate in this chapter? What impact do these strategies have on the viewpoints' persuasiveness? Explain, citing from the viewpoints.

Chapter 3

1. In the preface to this chapter, the anthology's editor explains that historically people have often reacted with fear to new technologies. Early in the eighteenth century, the Faculty of Medicine and Theology at the University of Paris opposed smallpox inoculation based upon their fears that inoculation was an uncharted innovation and an attempt to play God. Do any of the viewpoints in this chapter reflect similar fears? Are new technologies more dangerous than older technologies therefore warranting such fears? Explain why or why not, citing the viewpoints.

2. Jonathan L. Tempte believes that the human papillomavirus (HPV) vaccine is an excellent tool to fight the costly, deadly disease. Arthur Allen argues that the HPV vaccine should not be made mandatory until further evidence of its safety and effectiveness are available. Which argument do you find more persuasive? Explain.

Chapter 4

1. Which of the strategies, technologies, or policies in this chapter do you believe will have the greatest impact on the future of medicine? Explain your answer, citing from the texts.

2. According to Bruce L. Flamm, studies show that intercessory prayer has no medicinal benefits. Father Tom Ryan claims that these studies cannot measure God's healing power. Both authors use very different rhetorical strategies and have very different affiliations. How does each author's affiliation influence his rhetoric? Do you think this makes one viewpoint more persuasive than the other? Explain why or why not, citing from the viewpoints.

3. Albert de la Chapelle argues that genetic testing will save lives. Henry T. Greeley agrees, but is concerned about

how those tests might be used. Do you think de la Chapelle's assurances against discrimination are enough to allay Greeley's fears? Citing both viewpoints, explain why or why not.

4. Arthur Caplan believes human enhancement will improve humanity. Bryan Appleyard is unsure human enhancement will be a positive step. How do Caplan and Appleyard define human nature? How do these definitions influence their viewpoints? Explain.

Organizations to Contact

The editors have compiled the following list of organizations concerned with the issues debated in this book. The descriptions are derived from materials provided by the organizations. All have publications or information available for interested readers. The list was compiled on the date of publication of the present volume; the information provided here may change. Be aware that many organizations take several weeks or longer to respond to inquiries, so allow as much time as possible.

American Council on Science and Health
1995 Broadway, 2nd Fl., New York, NY   10023-5860
(866) 905-2694 • fax: (212) 362-4919
e-mail: acsh@acsh.org
Web site: www.acsh.org

The American Council on Science and Health (ACSH) is a consumer education group concerned with issues related to food, nutrition, chemicals, pharmaceuticals, lifestyle, the environment, and health. It publishes the quarterly newsletter *Priorities* and other reports, some of which are available on its Web site, including *The Top Ten Unfounded Health Scares of 2006* and *The Promise of Vaccines: The Science and the Controversy*.

American Medical Association
515 N. State St., Chicago, IL   60610
(312) 464-5000
Web site: www.ama-assn.org

The American Medical Association (AMA) is the largest professional association for medical doctors. It helps set standards for medical education and practices, and it is a powerful lobby in Washington, DC for physicians' interests. The association publishes specific journals for many medical fields and the AMA's prestigious weekly *Journal of the American Medical As-*

sociation. It also publishes a magazine of current issues important to physicians, the bimonthly *AMA Voice*, archives of which are available on its Web site. Also on its Web site, the AMA publishes speeches given by AMA leaders, including "U.S. Health Care System Reform and Ethical Issues in Health Care."

American Public Health Association

800 I St. NW, Washington, DC   20001-3710
(202) 777-APHA • fax: (202) 777-2533
e-mail: comments@apha.org
Web site: www.apha.org

Founded in 1872, the American Public Health Association (APHA) consists of over 50,000 individuals and organizations that aim to improve public health. Its members represent over fifty public health occupations, including researchers, practitioners, administrators, teachers, and other health care workers. APHA publishes books, including *Race and Research*. Other APHA publications include the monthly newspaper *The Nation's Health* and the *American Journal of Public Health*, recent issues of which are available on the Web site.

Center for Bioethics

University of Pennsylvania, Philadelphia, PA   19104
(215) 898-7136 • fax: (215) 573-3036
Web site: www.bioethics.upenn.edu

The Center of Bioethics at the University of Pennsylvania is the largest bioethics center in the world, and it runs the world's first and largest bioethics Web site. Faculty at the center conduct research on issues including human research and experimentation, genetic testing, and transplantation. Its Web site www.bioethic.net is home of *The American Journal of Bioethics* *(AJOB)*, the Center's flagship electronic journal, which includes articles and commentary on medical ethics issues. Current and some past issues are available on the Web site.

Council for Responsible Genetics

5 Upland Rd., Suite 3, Cambridge, MA   02140

(617) 868-0870 • fax: (617) 491-5344
e-mail: crg@gene-watch.org
Web site: www.gene-watch.org

The Council for Responsible Genetics is a national organization of scientists, health professionals, trade unionists, women's health activists, and others who work to ensure that biotechnology is developed safely and in the public interest. The council publishes the book *Rights and Liberties in the Biotech Age*, position papers on the Human Genome Project, genetic discrimination, germ-line modifications, and DNA-based identification systems. The Council also publishes the bimonthly magazine *GeneWatch*, recent issues of which are available on its Web site. Also on its Web site are articles and position papers, including "Misleading Marketing of Genetic Tests" and the "Genetic Discrimination."

The Hastings Center
21 Malcolm Gordon Road, Garrison, NY   10524-4125
(845) 424-4040 • fax: (845) 424-4545
e-mail: mail@thehastingscenter.org
Web site: www.thehastingscenter.org

The Hastings Center is an independent research institute that explores the medical, ethical, and social ramifications of the health care system and medical advances. The Center publishes books, such as *Medicine and the Market: Equity v. Choice*, papers, guidelines, and the bimonthly *Hastings Center Report*, selected articles from which are available on its Web site. Also on the Web site are the reports *Genetic Differences and Human Identities* and *Is Better Always Good? The Enhancement Project*.

Healthcare Leadership Council
1001 Pennsylvania Avenue, NW, Washington, DC   20004
(202) 452-8700 • fax: (202) 296-9561
Web site: www.hlc.org

The Healthcare Leadership Council (HLC) is a forum in which health care industry leaders can jointly develop policies, plans, and programs that support a market-based health care system.

HLC believes America's health care system should value innovation and provide affordable high-quality health care free from excessive government regulations. On its Web site, HLC publishes the latest press releases on health issues and newsletter articles, including "Medical Liability Crisis Continues to Put Providers, Patients at Risk" and "Evidence on Government-Run Health Systems Mounts."

The Kennedy Institute of Ethics
Georgetown University, Washington, DC   20057
(202) 687-8099 • fax: (202) 687-8089
Web site: http://kennedyinstitute.georgetown.edu

The Kennedy Institute of Ethics sponsors research on medical ethics, including ethical issues surrounding the use of recombinant DNA and human gene therapy. The Institute publishes an annual bibliography in addition to reports and articles on bioethics issues. Its Library & Information Services link provides access to a variety of searchable medical and bioethics databases.

National Center for Complementary and Alternative Medicine
9000 Rockville Pike, Bethesda, MD   20892
(301) 519-3153 • fax: (866) 464-3616
e-mail: info@nccam.nih.gov
Web site: http://nccam.nih.gov

Congress established the National Center for Complementary and Alternative Medicine (NCCAM) (part of the U.S. National Institutes of Health) in 1998 to encourage and support research on complementary and alternative medicine (CAM). The center also provides information on CAM to health care providers and the public, evaluates the safety and effectiveness of popular herbal remedies and practices such as acupuncture, and supports studies to determine how CAM products interact with standard medications. NCCAM publishes consensus reports and fact sheets on various alternative treatments, cancer, and dietary supplements, some of which are available on its Web site.

National Coalition on Health Care
1200 G Street, NW, Washington, DC   20005
(202) 638-7151
e-mail: info@nchc.org
Web site: www.nchc.org

The National Coalition on Health Care is a nonprofit, nonpartisan group that represents the nation's largest alliance working to improve America's health care and make it more affordable. On its Web site the coalition publishes articles, reports, and speeches, including *Medical Errors and Improving Patient Safety* and *Impacts of Health Care Reform: Projections of Costs and Savings.*

National Institutes of Health
9000 Rockville Pike, Bethesda, MD   20892
(301) 496-4000
e-mail: nihinfo@od.nih.gov
Web site: www.nih.gov

The National Institutes of Health (NIH) (part of the U.S. Department of Health and Human Services) is comprised of twenty-seven separate components, including the National Human Genome Research Institute and the National Cancer Institute. The NIH's mission is to discover new knowledge that will improve health. In order to achieve this mission, the NIH conducts and supports research, helps train research investigators, and fosters the communication of medical information. The NIH also publishes on-line fact sheets, brochures, and handbooks.

National Women's Health Information Center
8270 Willow Oaks Corporate Drive, Fairfax, VA   22031
(800) 994-9662
Web site: www.4woman.gov

The National Women's Health Information Center (NWIHC) is a service of the Office on Women's Health in the U.S. Department of Health and Human Services. It provides access to current and reliable information on a wide array of women's health issues. The organization publishes a monthly newsletter, *Healthy Women Today*, past issues of which are available on its Web site as are other NWIHC resources, including "Common Screening and Diagnostic Tests and Screening Tests" and "Immunizations Guidelines for Women."

Quackwatch
P.O. Box 1747, Allentown, PA   18105
(610) 437-1795
e-mail: sbinfo@quackwatch.com
Web site: www.quackwatch.com

Quackwatch is a nonprofit organization that combats health-related frauds and fads. Its activities include reporting illegal marketing of medical-related products, improving the quality of health information available on the Internet, and distributing reliable publications. The Web site has reports on topics including herbal medicine, homeopathy, and other alternative treatments.

United Network for Organ Sharing
700 North 4th Street, Richmond, VA   23219
(804) 782-4800 • fax: (804) 782-4817
Web site: www.unos.org

The United Network for Organ Sharing (UNOS) is a system of transplant and organ procurement centers, tissue-typing labs, and transplant surgical teams. It was formed to help organ donors and people who need organs to find each other. By federal law, organs used for transplants must be cleared through UNOS. The network also formulates and implements national policies on equal access to organs and organ allocation, organ procurement, and AIDS testing. It publishes the monthly *UNOS Update*. On its Web site, UNOS publishes fact sheets, white papers, and brochures.

U.S. Centers for Disease Control and Prevention— National Office of Public Health Genomics

4770 Buford Hwy., Mailstop K–89, Atlanta, GA   30341-3724
(770) 488-8510 • fax: (770) 488-8355
e-mail: genetics@cdc.gov
Web site: www.cdc.gov/genomics

The National Office of Public Health Genomics (NOPHG) at the U.S. Centers for Disease Control and Prevention provides leadership and coordinates efforts among other federal agencies, public health organizations, professional groups, and the private sector to raise awareness of genetics and disease prevention. Its Web site provides updated information on how human genomic discoveries can be used to improve health and prevent disease. NOPHG publishes *Genomics & Health Weekly Update*, recent issues of which are available on its Web site. The sites Genetic Testing link provides access to articles, position papers, and reports, including *Your Genes, Your Choices.*

Bibliography of Books

Nicholas Agar   *Liberal Eugenics: In Defence of Human Enhancement.* Malden, MA: Blackwell, 2005.

Harold W. Baillie and Timothy K. Casey, eds.   *Is Human Nature Obsolete?: Genetics, Bioengineering, and the Future of the Human Condition.* Cambridge, MA: MIT Press, 2005.

Alan W. Bock   *Waiting to Inhale: The Politics of Medical Marijuana.* Santa Ana, CA: Seven Locks, 2000.

Michael Carlston   *Classical Homeopathy.* New York: Churchill Livingstone, 2003.

Audrey R. Chapman and Mark S. Frankel, eds.   *Designing Our Descendants: The Promises and Perils of Genetic Modifications.* Baltimore, MD: Johns Hopkins University Press, 2003.

Robert I. Field   *Health Care Regulation in America: Complexity, Confrontation, and Compromise.* New York: Oxford University Press, 2007.

Francis Fukuyama   *Our Posthuman Future: Consequences of the Biotechnology Revolution.* New York: Farrar, Straus, and Giroux, 2002.

Rudolph J. Gerber   *Legalizing Marijuana: Drug Policy Reform and Prohibition Politics.* Westport, CT: Praeger, 2004.

Kenneth W. Goodman	*Ethics and Evidence-Based Medicine: Fallibility and Responsibility in Clinical Science.* New York: Cambridge University Press, 2003.
Tom Heller, Geraldine Lee-Treweek, Jeanne Katz, Julie Stone, and Sue Spurr, eds.	*Perspectives on Complementary and Alternative Medicine.* New York: Routledge, 2005.
Ana Smith Iltis	*Research Ethics.* New York: Routledge, 2006.
Institute of Medicine	*Financing Vaccines in the 21st Century: Assuring Access and Availability.* Washington, DC: National Academies Press, 2004
Maxwell J. Mehlman	*Wondergenes: Genetic Enhancement and the Future of Society.* Bloomington: Indiana University Press, 2003.
Ramez Naam	*More Than Human: Embracing the Promise of Biological Enhancement.* New York: Broadway Books, 2005.
J. Odorico, S.C. Zhang, and R. Pedersen, eds.	*Human Embryonic Stem Cells.* New York: Garland Science/BIOS Scientific Publishers, 2005.
Andrea Farkas Patenaude	*Genetic Testing for Cancer: Psychological Approaches for Helping Patients and Families.* Washington, DC: American Psychological Association, 2004.

William M. Sage and Rogan Kersh, eds.   *Medical Malpractice and the U.S. Health Care System.* New York: Cambridge University Press, 2004.

Carlos Simón and Antonio Pellicer, eds.   *Stem Cells in Human Reproduction: Basic Science and Therapeutic Potential.* Abingdon, UK: Informa Healthcare, 2007.

Brian D. Smedley, Adrienne Y. Stith, and Alan R. Nelson, eds.   *Unequal Treatment: Confronting Racial and Ethnic Disparities in Health Care.* Washington, DC: National Academy Press, 2003.

Daniel P. Sulmasy   *The Rebirth of the Clinic: An Introduction to Spirituality in Health Care.* Washington, DC: Georgetown University Press, 2006.

Philip Tovey, Gary Easthope, and Jon Adams, eds.   *The Mainstreaming of Complementary and Alternative Medicine: Studies in Social Context.* New York: Routledge, 2004.

Index